The Importance of Not Having a Career Plan

The Importance of Not Having a Career Plan

Glenn Martin

G.P. MARTIN PUBLISHING

Published 2026 by G.P. Martin Publishing

Website: www.glennmartin.com.au

Contact: info@glennmartin.com.au

Book layout and cover design by the author.

Typeset in Sitka 11 pt

Printed by Lulu.com

ISBN: 978 1 7644114 3 1 (pbk.)

A catalogue record for this book is available from the National Library of Australia

Contents

PART 1: A WORKING LIFE WITHOUT A CAREER PLAN 1

Chapter 1: Vocational guidance 1

Chapter 2: A career revised 8

Chapter 3: After teaching 21

Chapter 4: Working in the community 31

Chapter 5: Back to university 42

Chapter 6: The real apprenticeship... 52

Chapter 7: Veering into training and instructional design......... 66

PART 2: BEING A WRITER (OR NOT) 75

Chapter 8: The child chooses to be a writer 75

Chapter 9: The adult earns a livelihood...................................... 86

Chapter 10: Writing comes to the fore 97

PART 3: WAYS OF NOT HAVING A CAREER PLAN........................ 107

Chapter 11: Fundamentals of career planning 107

Chapter 12: Creative people without careers 124

Chapter 13: Careers and mythology 136

Afterword 145

References 146

Author profile.. 147

Other books by Glenn Martin 148

PART 1: A WORKING LIFE WITHOUT A CAREER PLAN

Chapter 1: Vocational guidance

When I was in high school, vocational guidance had become a trend. I was a high-achieving scholar and a dutiful child, although with an undertone of rebelliousness. How would this play out?

I was brought up to think that I would find a place in society as an intelligent and educated young man. It was the post-war years, and everything was full steam ahead.

But I did not find vocational guidance helpful. I went to see the vocational guidance counsellor at school. I undertook various kinds of tests. I was told that my intelligence was high, above that of most of my high school comrades. I was given pamphlets about various professions, with the inference that I could pursue any of them if I wished: doctor, lawyer, engineer, surveyor, teacher.

All of these professions seemed a long way removed from my life or anything I was familiar with. My mother sent me to a Vocational Guidance Bureau in the city. I did a lot more tests there, At the end of it all, I had an interview with a man. He had some news for me: I could do anything I set my mind to. I had the intelligence for any of it.

And he had more pamphlets, mostly the same ones, but it didn't matter. What did I want to do? I still had no idea. I had no familiarity with any of these professions (except for teaching).

So, through high school, I was wrestling with career choices. It was imperative that I acquire an occupation or, most likely, a profession. I was part of the post-war generation, with its momentum and its technological rush. There was a role for me to play there if I set myself to work at it, but I felt like the veritable blank slate.

There was a primary divide in vogue: science or the arts, technology or philosophy. My problem was, I had the ability to do either. Apparently, it wasn't usually this way; a student was supposed to be good at one or the other or at least, interested in one or the other. I was not so much interested in biology, but I enjoyed physics, so science was of interest to me.

It was also easier to see how I could forge a career in this direction. I could be an engineer. I could even make a choice as to what kind of engineer I wanted to be. The main one seemed to be civil engineering, but there was also electrical, mechanical, chemical, and mining. Later, I discovered there were many other more precise avenues: electronics, audio-engineering, materials science and manufacturing, hydraulics, construction.

However, I was also interested in writing, and I was writing poetry. After I had written a poem, I would write it out neatly in an exercise book I had acquired for the purpose. Eventually I filled it up, and I started another. By the end of high school, I had several of these books, and I accepted it as a part of me, an important part. I was sensible enough to know there was no career in this. Even famous poets, like Keats, did not make a living out of being a poet.

I had to keep reminding myself of this cruel fact of the world, and remind myself that I needed to earn a living. That was the fundamental fact. I had no fanciful illusions that the world should provide for me so that I could sit around writing poems for their entertainment. I was prepared to be realistic, practical and hard-working.

Nevertheless, there had to be some attraction in the work. When the quest to find this becomes discouraging, it can be good to start at the other end. At least there are some things you can say that you are definitely not interested in. I didn't want to be a businessman, or a live performer, I didn't want to be a lawyer or an accountant. I didn't want to be a doctor. I wasn't going to be a painter, my father's occupation, because I wanted to have a job that required higher education.

Accordingly, I had ruled out all the trades: carpenter, plumber, plasterer, bus-driver, train-driver, truck driver, taxi-driver, mechanic, printer, cabinetmaker, hairdresser. I wasn't interested in going to sea, so sailor, first mate, ship's engineer and ship captain were ruled out. Salesperson, real estate agent, trader or auctioneer were not for me. And I wasn't going to go and live in the country, so farmer, stock & station agent, shearer, cattle farmer, dairy farmer, wheat farmer or fruit grower were not on my list of possibilities.

I liked this list. In one sense it was meaningless. I wasn't learning anything new and I wasn't refining any decision-making process. But, I was refining my sense of my place in the world, and I have come to appreciate the importance of context in our lives. This casual process also allowed me to cast my view over my family, such as I knew it then.

My father was a painter, in the days when it was admirable to end up with a trade as opposed to being kicked around the workforce picking up odd jobs all your life. My mother also worked: she was a dressmaker, and that had been something that ran in her family among the women. I didn't know many other men in either my mother's or my father's family. My mother had a brother who had invented a tap for petrol, as in petrol bowsers, and he had started a factory to produce them. He was successful, with both an engineering mind and a business mind. But he was an exception in the family.

My mother and father both had more siblings, but we never saw much of them, and I had no idea what jobs they had. And, as we were told, it didn't matter anyway, because the world had changed, and we would do something new, that required education. We would have new opportunities, and we would be some kind of professional. It didn't matter what.

My father died when I was in Year Twelve. He had a heart attack and died one afternoon. In the background floated the idea that it was the jobs of working class men that killed them, through poisons (had it been lead in paint that had hardened my father's arteries?), or bad air in the lungs, or physical exertion that was just too much. It was just the way things had been. But for us, it was all the more reason to become a professional. There would be no dying in a mine shaft, or in a hospital bed in our early fifties. And it was not as if these deaths were the fault of the men themselves. My father could not be blamed for drinking too much, smoking too much or fighting too much. He did none of these.

With my father dead, the same difficulty remained, only with more intensity: what should I do?

Time runs out. Difficulties do not resolve themselves simply because time passes. I reached the end of high school still with a decision to make. I did have a default answer, because of course people asked me what I was going to be. In desperation I said I was going to become a mathematics teacher. I was good at maths so it was a plausible story. In high school I continued to think on it, and my other answer became: civil engineer. It likewise sounded plausible: achievable and respectable, so much better than "I don't know".

I still wrote poetry. I did not publicise the fact.

I opted for engineering. It was the braver choice; it was something new. I went to university and started. But I found it difficult. I could do it, but it took my brain an immense effort, and there was very little left over. I tried to still write poetry, but it was even a struggle to shift from one type of thinking to another, and each one felt so ridiculous to the other. I felt schizophrenic, as if I were being torn apart.

I was still attending church at this time, and I was approached to go to an open night at a theological college. It was a very gentlemanly affair. Gentlemen from the college spoke about what we would study at the college, the course of training that was followed. It was related to theology, a perspective on the Bible, and the church's history. The upshot was also discussed: what happened if one completed the course? Did one go on to a career in the church as a chaplain, vicar, rector, minister?

Was it even appropriate to call it a career, since you had been picked out by God to do His service? What did it mean to be chosen by God? My understanding, after this session, was that one examined oneself to see if one heard God's voice calling you, and you told your minister or someone at the college about it. I didn't know what this would sound like. It sounded like voices in the night that could just as easily be illusions, or delusions.

I felt that I had to remain practical, and I also had to keep my eye on the necessary goal: earning a living. In one way it would have been a resolution to enter the ministry. It would have been a choice made that would result in some kind of a living, so I would never have to worry about that again. But I also felt an obligation to be independent, and to potentially provide for my mother, if she needed it. I couldn't see the ministry as enabling me to do that.

Having thought these things over in this way, I definitely did not hear the voice of God calling me to the ministry. I didn't think that I wanted to belong to the church in this way in any case. Even if I remained aligned with it, I didn't want to depend on it for my living. I was beginning to question the entailments of belonging. I had many questions, and I didn't think the institution would be sympathetic to my questions. I harboured them alone.

Accordingly, I studied engineering with a heavy heart. I could do the work, but it gave me no life. Would it ever be thus? When I wasn't learning my lessons, I spent time in the university library looking at the linkages between poetry and mathematics. It was an arid exploration. It wasn't as if I wanted to study the literature of poetry and mathematics, if I could even fathom a meaning for that association.

The poetry I wrote at this time was more urgent and anguished. It wasn't just me. Disruption was in the air. The student body had become fervent as well as righteous. There were plenty of people who had flags to fly and wanted to gather people around a cause. There were fevered conversations here and there, all over the city, but often the conversation was not so great: minds were made up, minds were outraged. It was hard to reconcile with any kind of day job.

Was it the Vietnam War? Was it capitalism? Was it godlessness or youthful waywardness? Or was it everything that was wrong? Was our entire modern life catastrophic?

In the midst, I tried to maintain connections. I had a motorbike. I visited my old school. The headmaster saw me and wanted to talk. I wasn't sure why. He had never engaged in much conversation when we were in school. He was located down the corridor, not supercilious but certainly aloof, and he had not spoken much to the senior pupils. But this time he invited me into his office and closed the door.

When I sat down, he said, "Glenn, what's going on? I see pictures of students in the streets, demonstrations, angry posters, barricading of the corridors in universities. What is happening?"

How could I have an answer to that? I was one person in the maelstrom. Many of these other students had objectives, I could see that. I think they smelled personal advantage, not just social reform. Some of them, at least, wanted power. I didn't.

I felt for the headmaster. At the end of his working life, it must have seemed as if everything was falling apart. And what for? It was hard to see a clear problem, harder still to see a clear solution. Of course there were problems: people are imperfect, societies are imperfect. Some systems are so bad that you wouldn't want to be part of them. Some of those systems are very big systems, like capitalism, but what can you do about that? What would you conceivably replace it with, and how?

I think what I said to the headmaster was that a lot of people were expressing dissatisfaction with many institutions, not just universities. And when there is a fervent of energy for change, it is best to see what can be accommodated, for the improvement of society as a whole. I may have seemed like a vacuous politician, but I would have been prepared to chair the meeting and demand that the parties listen to one another. But I was small, and I only had a small voice.

I was informed, about twelve months later, that the headmaster had died, in his last year in office. It was a heart attack. The deputy headmaster succeeded him. He was bolder.

All this was happening, and classes at university continued. Examinations took place. I was holding my future in abeyance, just being determined not to fail at this point. Failure is hard to drag after you. It meant I had to study hard, because it didn't come easily. Even in mathematics, which I had enjoyed through high school, I felt that I had peaked. What I had done was as much as I ever wanted to do in mathematics.

I had done algebra and I had done calculus in high school, and now someone had made equations out of calculus expressions. It sounded preposterous. I couldn't see how I could hold all that in my head. Later, when I had time to think about it, I came to the conclusion that other students knew that they didn't need to hold it all in their head. They had some mnemonic method of simplifying it, so they could get to the end without exhausting their brain. I think I missed out on learning such things.

Yet, that was probably an indication that this was not my natural territory. But someone has to do this stuff; society needs engineers. I had a high intellect, and I should take up the burden.

Many years later, people have said to me, "This was all happening in the couple of years after your father died. How did you feel?" Well, I was carrying on. I had to carry on. I had to learn a job so that I could earn money and be independent, as quickly as possible. I had to be responsible.

Chapter 2: A career revised

I lasted two years in the engineering degree. I made it to the end of the second year, and I passed all subjects. I got Distinctions in Physics, Mechanics of Solids, and Engineering Construction. In some subjects I got Credits, in some subjects I got Passes, and in Geotechnics I got a "Pass Conceded". That was alright, I thought. It was good enough. I wouldn't be returning to that particular pursuit. I had done well enough on the whole. (I had done two units of mathematics, first year and second year. I got a Credit in both units.)

I left the course. It was one of my first brave decisions in life. The factor that had swung things for me was the realisation that after I finished my four years of studying engineering, I would have to work at being an engineer for the next forty years. Yes, I know this is obvious, but sometimes you need to actually say it to yourself in order to appreciate the impact of it. I realised I could not go the next forty years being an engineer. Come what may, I had to find something else.

I looked around. I carved a space between me and the student movement. I realised that the students who were crying out for people to make a commitment to the cause would most likely have an exit plan for themselves in due course. I looked at them. They were for the most part the sons and daughters of rich people. They were used to getting their own way and they would make friends among others who were similarly rich and influential. And they could change their spots overnight if it served their purposes. The Establishment they were deriding today they would soon be part of themselves, happily. (And in years to come, it did turn out to be so. That's fine. I figure it was how those people liked to play, on both sides of the fence. But I did not wish to participate.)

My career plan had to be made up on the run, but it should not make a fool of me. I decided on teaching. I figured I had enough mathematics to get me halfway into a maths teachers' course. I wasn't really interested in teaching science. I did wonder about teaching English, but for that I would have had to go back to the beginning. I had already "wasted" two years. By going into a teaching course, I could salvage all of that waste.

How did I feel? Teaching was not my intended career, but it was something that I thought I could learn how to do. After all, it's the one occupation that we have all watched models of for twelve years by the time we have left school. So, why was it not my intended career? I was good at mathematics; I could certainly teach it. And I was good at English; I could teach that, too.

One issue was the way of the world. People didn't teach maths and English. They taught one or the other. If I said I wanted to teach both, it would be a constant fight with the hierarchy and the school as an organisation. I knew that the expectation would be that I would go away and think it over, and decide on one or the other. I didn't want to do that.

Perhaps my problem was that I was obstinate. Why didn't I go away and think it over, and make a decision? Because I didn't want to. I thought, this is what's wrong with the organisation, and the education system. It doesn't understand why I would want to do both. I wasn't about to resign my desire that embraced both maths and English. It was fundamental to include both in one's person.

These little places of obstinacy can determine the direction of one's life.

I would hear about a person like Leonardo da Vinci, and how he was a polymath, and think that I had wide interests too. But I wasn't saying I was a genius like him. I was saying I was normal, both he and I were normal. But people's view about this subject was that da Vinci lived a long time ago in a different society. We live in a modern society where people have jobs: maths teachers and English teachers. I needed to align myself with what was given, because that was the only way I would get a job.

The corollary of such conversations was: if you're unhappy, get a hobby. You write poetry? Good. Write it down in a book. Take up a sport as well.

I gave up at this point. I went to teachers' college and studied being a mathematics teacher. There was a fast track for people who had bailed out of a university course. The Education Department didn't mind because they were short of teachers, and providing a fast track was cheaper than attracting teachers from overseas (which they did as well). They could encourage us by offering us an extra year's qualification, and a small pay increment, after we had taught for them for several years.

The shortcoming of my new career plan was that for me, it wasn't a long-term plan. In fact, I didn't have a long-term plan. I knew I didn't want to get locked in for the long term to teaching, because teaching was not part of my career goals.

Not that I had even had career goals. The truth was, I still did not know what I wanted to be, no more now than when I was thirteen, or fourteen, or fifteen. I just knew that I needed to earn a living, and I liked to write poetry. I understood that this was in my spare time. And it wasn't just poetry; I liked to write. I liked the process of thinking and articulating ideas. They could be reports, plans, essays, ideas, on all aspects of life. There was an influence aspect as well. I wanted to be able to express things that influenced the way people thought and felt.

At one stage (around eight years old) I thought I could be a writer of messages on cards: birthday cards, Christmas cards, sympathy cards. I liked the idea of writing something cheerful, or soothing, or insightful. I appreciate now that it takes a great deal of wisdom to write helpful messages to people. Then, it seemed like an unreachable goal anyway, some undefined job in some undefinable company, and I didn't know how one would approach such a job or prepare for it. Was it even a real job?

And was it a consequential job anyway? I wanted to do something important.

What I remember from that time is that I wanted to do something that was helpful to others, in the way words were used. In the years after that, I worked at learning about words: new words and their meanings, different contexts for words, social meanings, different groups of people and how they connected with each other. So many things we need to learn, before we even think about how we could fulfil a job in society.

How does one devise a career plan as a young person? And indeed, is that a meaningful or worthwhile thing to do? I would start by asking, what is obvious?

A few things might be obvious. For example, if your father (or your mother) is a doctor and the expectation is that you become a doctor, "to continue the tradition", then that might settle things. Let's say you are quite happy to become a doctor. You understand the field, its purpose, what it requires of you, and the lifestyle that it will lead to, and you have no quarrel with any of it. You have the capability, and you are prepared to do the work.

In this context, devising a career plan is almost superfluous. There might be nuances that indicate your personal preferences. You would like to be an orthopaedic surgeon rather than a general practitioner.

There is also the opposite situation, where a parent has an established calling and they expect you to follow the same calling, but you don't want to do that. And there is a struggle over it. You either relent and accept the pathway grudgingly, or you fight. And fights within families can be like fights to the death. Even then there are two situations.

You may have a very clear alternative idea of your career, or you may not; you may just know that you do not want to do the traditional, accepted thing. The second situation is like mine. I knew I didn't want to be aimless and useless, and there were many, many occupations that I did not want to occupy, even if I were to be excellent at them.

To take the situation where you know the direction you want to go, you are just lacking the support for it, you still have to ask yourself how realistic it is. There are plenty of dreamers out there shouting advice from the sidelines: "Seize the day!" However, the truth is somewhat more delicate, or subtle. For a start, it is your truth, not anyone else's, and it is certainly not a general truth. And your life has not been lived before, so patterns from the past are only of limited value.

You might say you'd like to be a poet, novelist, artist, singer. These are not jobs. We live in an industrial economy, so there are some contexts where such activities can be made into jobs, but the essential truth is that they are not jobs. No one will pay you to produce such fare on a regular basis. A job as a singer might be a regular spot in a club, but it is a mistake to apply the paradigm of "job" to artistic activities in general. Our heads are filled with the exceptions: the writer who gets paid $1 million for each novel. But they are the exceptions.

It is important to expunge such conceptions from our minds. They invariably slide into the expectation that society owes you a living, or that people should buy your paintings. These attitudes do not move us one tiny step closer towards achieving our career goal.

What is a career goal?

There are phases of this exploration, and different aspects. An easy career goal is an occupation, trade or profession that will earn you sufficient money to live well (nice house, nice furniture, nice car, holidays, entertainment). It will also give you an accepted place in society: respect.

You may also desire this goal but find it difficult to achieve. It might take twenty years of hard work and strategising instead of it being an easy ride. Within that package of achievements, you may have different priorities (for example, travel may be important to you).

One also has to see one's life as a whole. The spheres of work, place of living, personal relationships, activities outside of work: all of these things are important and interdependent, not separate. They may not be directly connected, but they are interdependent; they depend on each other and affect each other. The dependence may be economic, or related to time, or it may be emotional, or depend on relationships.

The choices we make in all of these areas do not have to be subservient to the job we have, unless that is what is most important to us, and we have our reasons. A career plan may be the most important thing in a book on career planning, but a career plan may not be the most important thing in a book on a philosophy of life.

This is not a book on career planning, although some useful things might be said about career planning.

A career goal would seem to come first. We have to see that a career goal is a subset of a life goal. And what is a life goal? We could say it is about your destiny. Perhaps it is not fashionable to wrestle with the idea of destiny these days. We have no destiny; there is just life, and we live it as best we can. Or, is it that only some special people have a destiny? Such as, Mahatma Ghandi was destined to lead India to independence.

But, we are here, and few of us are great leaders, so, is there destiny for modest people too? What would it be? We know, as we grow up, that we grow into capability, and the world is a place where capabilities can be exercised. And we see that there are needs in the world. I am assuming that we are looking beyond selfishness and greed. To look for one's destiny is to look for a part that one can play in the world, a useful or delightful part.

Is there something we were meant to do or be? What if we don't like this language? What if it seems inappropriate today? It seems rigid, and it seems to imply that a being external to the world is pre-ordaining what is going to (or should) happen in life. This kind of thinking seems to belong to yesterday, to a fixed, hierarchical world. Can we live without it?

Let's say we can. The point of a career goal and a career plan would be to give some direction to your life, so that you don't wander aimlessly. That much makes sense. There is a point of balance we can strive for. One side is being aimless, which means that we do not develop our talents in a coherent way. The other side is to be too rigid, fixing all the steps we will take and sticking to them rigidly, even when it no longer makes sense.

An example would be aiming to become a lamplighter and charting out all the steps towards that goal, then finding out that someone had invented the electric light. (I had an ancestor who was a lamplighter, so I am entitled to use this example.) In this case, sticking rigidly to the plan would not be helpful. Unfortunately, many situations that we might find ourselves in are as futile as this. We need to continue to review our plans for their viability and relevance. We need to be ready to adapt.

And yet, here is a challenging statement: **Live long enough to fulfil your destiny.**

There is something inspiring about this statement. Can we take the "destiny" out of it? Yes, we can, but there are two parts to it. First, live long enough to fulfil your potential, and second, live long enough to achieve some good in the world through the use of your capabilities.

Now, destiny is not some exalted thing, but something within your reach, at least, within reach of your "better self". It is human, something you can do if you give yourself to it and apply the effort. And there is wisdom in it. It will be in line with your capabilities and interests, your talents. It has two qualities: it will not twist you out of shape, and it will not harm others.

Here is something you can work with. But still we might be discouraged. Why don't this goal and this pathway become immediately clear? Why wasn't my course in life clear to me in the teenage years?

To take a little example, suppose I had decided to become a writer of messages on greeting cards. I would not have had the maturity at the end of high school to step right into that that. So, how could I have prepared myself? That's a question for you. What could I have done?

Any number of things. I could have got a job as a shop assistant, or as a helper in a community centre, to get some experience of people and their ordinary lives. I could have studied psychology to try to understand what makes people feel bad or good. I could have become a journalist, as a way of experiencing life and writing about it regularly.

The general point is that some jobs are not for the young and inexperienced. They might not even seem relevant until you have some experience. This is another reason not to have a career plan. You don't have enough knowledge or experience at the moment.

An example: I have met management consultants whose background you would never guess. The starkest example was a man who had been a chemical engineer. How did he get from one role to the other? The answer is, not suddenly. He carried out projects where different aspects of the work presented themselves as issues: planning aspects, relationships between people, where he gradually came to see that he could offer something helpful. Gradually, people came to ask this of him. They no longer needed his skills as a chemical engineer. And he discovered that he was enjoying this new work.

Did he need to visit a vocational guidance counsellor during this period? Well, some kind of counsellor might have been helpful to him to talk through his transition, but it wasn't likely that he could have planned this transition at the beginning of his career. He had to go through the experience as it presented itself to him. His talent was to be aware of the different aspects of his situation, and to imagine different possibilities for his life.

Career transitions, or their possibility, may reveal themselves over time, and what reveals itself will be in keeping with your current capacity and development.

But there is also something about career development and transitions that has to do with right and wrong. What you strive to do must be for the good of all-that-is. It may be to bring out what is within you. It may be to contribute to the common good, to people and the natural world. And it is a holistic endeavour: one good thing does not make up for a myriad of improper things.

The beginning of a career is when we decide to impose a direction on our life. An example: a young man had gone overseas for twelve months, then come home and wandered into a succession of jobs in call centres. The jobs were satisfactory, but not satisfying. After a few years of this, he decided to go to college and learn graphic design. He imposed a direction on his life, weighing up the purpose, the costs and the likely rewards. He completed the course of study and began a career as a graphic designer.

In my case, I completed my one year of teachers' college and began teaching. I had achieved one goal: I was earning a living as a professional. It was not my preferred work, but I didn't know what that was, so it was okay for now. And I had kept another option open. At the same time that I transferred to teachers' college, I started an Arts degree. I decided to major in education and philosophy. I did the Arts course part-time, so the study continued after I started teaching.

I had a great deal to learn in order to survive as a teacher. I had seen other young teachers not handle the classroom well, and bail out before twelve months were up. For me it was a big struggle. For one thing, I preferred to work by myself. Lots of jobs would have suited me better: surveyor, architect, journalist, engineer, printer – almost anything except constantly interacting with other people, especially children! And one had to do it all day, constantly in front of a class full of children, many of whom didn't want to be there, and couldn't see anything attractive about my performance that made them want to be there. And I was teaching mathematics, the subject that most children love to hate.

Why did I persevere? It would have been no shame to give up. There were plenty of reasons to leave teaching. It was not as if I eventually wanted to be here, as my accepted career. But it's not true that there would have been no shame; there would have been. Added to that, I thought that if I failed at teaching, it implied that there were many other things I would fail at as well. Best to persevere; experience had to help.

Sometimes it is so; there are simple, practical things one has to learn, and it will take time. If you do not make the effort when the situation has presented itself to you, when will you? I went home close to tears every day, emotionally exhausted. I wasn't tall, and some of these children were taller than me. That didn't help. And I had to learn how to use my voice; it wasn't naturally loud.

At teachers' college, we were taught about lesson plans. But in those days, I often had eight different lessons in a day. How does one devise eight different lesson plans when one is already in front of a class all day? But that wasn't the primary difficulty. The big thing was "keeping control" of a class. What was the point of a lesson plan when the interruptions were constant and came from many different quarters?

It was also the days of physical punishment: the cane. The subject master offered to cane children for me. That should help, he said. I also realised that the cane was part of the culture: it was an expectation by all parties. It was part of the overall classroom performance: teachers and pupils in combat. But I didn't want to play.

I spent many days shouting most of the day. I went home with a ragged throat. I wasn't happy with myself, but I did accept the classroom situation as my problem to learn how to resolve. And I tried to do it within the classroom. I noticed some other teachers who were also struggling, coped by sending many children out of the classroom every lesson. I tried that too; it helped temporarily, but it was not fair on anybody.

I also had the thought that at the heart of it, the educational experience, there was something enjoyable. To take mathematics as an example, I think there is a magic about discovering algebra for the first time, and seeing what it enables you to do, and how you can play with it. I had to try and make the space where that realisation could happen.

There was also the challenge thrown at the hapless teacher by young high-schoolers: "What's the use of this, sir? Why do we have to learn this?" Eventually, I took this head-on, and I said to them in all earnestness: "Because if you don't know how to do elementary mathematics, people you have to deal with in life will mess you around, because they'll know you're ignorant. You need to learn this stuff."

This often helped. They could see that something serious was at stake, and they were blowing it away. We became comrades instead of adversaries. Who knows why we had to start out as adversaries? Was it their family, was it the suburb, was it about migration, being new in an unfamiliar, threatening country? It didn't matter; I just had to make a safe space where we could both do some useful work.

Occasionally I got an indication that I had made some inroads. An Aboriginal boy in one school said to me one day in the playground, jokingly, "You might be white, sir, but you're not a bad fella." He smiled. So did I.

At some point, someone made this statement to me: in teachers' college, you learn how to teach a subject, but you are never teaching a subject, you are teaching young people. You have to learn how to do that. It was a significant statement. Of course, there was a balance to be found between the two conceptions, and I had to work at that.

I spent three years teaching. There was a practical reason for this; I was on a three-year bond from teachers' college. At the end of this period, I also received my Teacher's Certificate. We fast-track people didn't get our certificate until we had served three years' teaching.

At this point, I was a little more confident in teaching, and I was not a disaster in a classroom.

I had learned many valuable skills through my perseverance. I would never have thought that I could "handle" a classroom and coax a group of young people through the learning process. I could manage a group and keep them focused. I could teach mathematical concepts and skills, dare I say, competently? I had begun to earn respect from pupils and fellow teachers as well.

I could have stayed. Was I ready to settle down and accept my fate, or was there still some unsatisfactory, unformed career plan nudging me? I think that fate is what you accept, while destiny (to use that language) is about an inner drive. Fate is a default position. You can allow it to seal itself over you. But destiny is something you can move yourself towards, or put yourself in the pathway of. Your actions can make a positive difference if they come from a strong motivation, and not from half-hearted whims.

It can be disturbing to talk about destiny, uncomfortable. One is just an ordinary, small person, looking for a way to earn a living. What does the universe care? And I am not much in the great scheme of things, so why should the universe care? But I don't have to look at it this way. I can think, instead, that I can choose to do this or that, so why wouldn't I do the most worthy thing? Why wouldn't I make the most of my possibility? Why wouldn't I seek to serve the good of all?

It is about what is possible for you, about your potential, but it is a little stronger than that, too. It is not just about what is possible, but about what you can make room for in front of you. It is as if you obtained a field of land, and your idea was to make a wonderful garden on it. You could make this happen if you really wanted to, and you applied the effort and the intelligence and the imagination to make it happen.

You would face setbacks and overcome them. You would create a garden of a high standard, something glorious, because that was your vision, and other people would recognise it. That is the kind of thinking we need to bring to career planning. If it is about destiny, it is a destiny that you make, not something that is gifted to you from on high, from the world of predestination.

Chapter 3: After teaching

I left teaching. Perhaps I should say also, there was a twelve-month period when I had a motorcycle accident, and I was thrown sideways from my life. One leg was broken badly, and it took a year to repair, before I was on my feet again. A large group of my students came into the hospital to see me, and they had to step a long way out of their world, out on the fringes of the city, to do so. There was a lot of love there. But although I was on the mend, my bond with them was broken.

Once I got out of hospital, another path would open up. I was still on crutches, and I worked temporarily at a high school close to where I lived, but at the end of the year, I left the teaching service. I was still pursuing a Bachelor of Arts, although the future pathway was not at all clear. I felt that it was in line with my inner drive. My attraction to words had extended into an attraction to ideas and to how learning occurs.

This was still very vague, but the guiding question was: is this **at least consistent with my inner drive**? I did not finish this university course either. The circumstances militated against it. I managed to finish two full years (successfully), and then the third year, which I started full-time, became a debacle. My subjects were philosophy and education, and I found them both engaging.

I studied traditional topics in philosophy: mind and body, consciousness, free will, ethics, perception, the existence of God, knowledge, existentialism, Marxism. We studied many well-known philosophers of Western philosophy. It was challenging to determine what stance to take on many of these issues, although what seemed to matter was to take a stance.

But, the School of Philosophy was disintegrating. There were three factions: Traditionalists, Marxists and Existentialists, and relations between them were so acrimonious that the university gave up and broke the school up into three discrete schools. To me, this was a failure of the university, and of the people involved. How was I supposed to make a choice in this environment? It seemed self-defeating.

Then there was Education. It likewise disintegrated, but in a different way. There was a rebellion, the gist of which was, "We don't like what you're teaching." How could I make a judgement like that? I didn't know much about the subject of education. I was not long out of high school. So were all the people around me.

The students had a big meeting. They decided they would run the school themselves and create their own courses within education. They asked for ideas about curriculum, and about teaching methods. At one level, I agreed. I was all for democratic involvement. But what if everyone is ignorant, and all of the received knowledge of the School of Education over generations was just thrown out the window as if it meant nothing?

The students had further meetings to decide on subjects they were interested in, how the teaching would occur and be assessed. I wondered, if this happened, what the degrees would be worth. Would they be recognised by the university? I already knew that if I wanted to learn something, I could do it myself. I could talk to people, visit a bookshop, find some relevant books, and study them. I couldn't imagine this happening here.

I felt a bit more distant about this turbulence. I had had a job and I could always go back there. I wasn't a helpless student fresh out of high school. I mulled this over for a couple of weeks, not prepared to make any unsatisfactory decisions. At the time, I was living with my girlfriend. And it was during this time that she announced she was pregnant. I did not hesitate. I said I would leave the university course and get a job. It was fine.

It was early enough in the year that for these two subjects, my academic record was marked "Discontinued, not to count as failure".

I took a job as a nurse in a psychiatric centre. How was this in line with a career plan, or even an "inner drive"? It seems wayward.

To explain that, I have to go back to the end of high school. Before I had made my decision to enter engineering, I toyed with studying everything. I wanted to know psychology, history, philosophy, education, sociology.... I was enthused about understanding everything in life.

By the time I had several years of university study under my belt, my concerns were more practical: I wanted to explore lots of different workplaces, that showed all different aspects of society. I was interested in how people with psychiatric problems were perceived, and how they were treated. I thought that in this way I could get a deeper understanding of society and could work out my stance towards it and where I wanted to fit into it.

If I wanted to relate my decision to my inner drive, I would have to say this was a long-range plan. But, many young people were going overseas at this time: to England, Europe, America, India, Bali. That was not my preference. I wanted to experience jobs that were hidden from normal view. I wanted to see what I would find there.

The psychiatric centre had a reputation for being a tough environment. Most of the wards were lock-up wards with long-term patients, meaning, they had been there for twenty or more years. The nurses were custodians, nothing else. We managed daily routines and tried to ensure there was no violence. In some of the other wards, people might eventually go home (suitably medicated), but in this ward, there was no such hope. Most of the patients did not have family who came to see them anymore.

The surrounding walls were sandstone, about fifteen feet high, around a large quadrangle. Many patients paced the concrete pathway around the yard. Some were sullen, some were manic, some had only a little speech, some had nervous tics. There was a common room with a large television screen bolted to the wall up high. The nurses had a room behind it, with a large screen of solid glass. We had many keys.

A highlight was morning and afternoon tea, when large slabs of cake would come out and be devoured. Order was paramount on these occasions, or it would quickly dissolve into an unholy ruckus. There were usually a few moments of contentedness while patients consumed their piece of cake. Sometimes, however, there would be a fight, and a scuffle, that marred the small interlude.

Medication was administered military-style. Patients were trained to be docile, and the medication made them more so. When I had time, usually during nightshift, I read many of the patients' files so I could understand the genesis of these people. How had this begun?

Because it was about thirty years after the end of the Second World War, there were a few men who had been broken by the war and who had not returned to be able to participate in normal social functioning. In some cases, they had brain damage. But mostly, their troubles had commenced when they were young men (yes, I was on the male ward; there was a female ward as well). They had had some kind of crisis in normal family and social situations.

I am not arguing that these "normal" situations were healthy, but once one person had been identified as mentally dysfunctional, that was the way it continued to be. The medical model was strong. Any crisis was met with medication and, not so long ago, on some occasions, with lobotomies. Some of the older nurses held the view that the surgery had been successful (bad parts of the brain had been removed), but the person had not been retrained properly. They had to be reconditioned into proper social patterns of behaviour.

Secretly, I was reading radical perspectives on psychiatry, and I had read *One Flew Over the Cuckoo's Nest* by Ken Kesey. I did not know what to do about the ideas that were forming in my mind. I could see that institutions involved the establishment and exercise of power, and to belong to an institution, one had to comply with the hierarchy of power. Indeed, one had to agree with the hierarchy. It was a much more extreme version of a school.

Looking back at the schools I had been at, I tried to see the differences and similarities between that and this. The schools were not environments I found congenial, and I thought I would like to see schools that were decidedly different, but at least I had been able to create small bubbles of harmonious atmosphere where constructive work could occur. I couldn't see any possibility of that in the psychiatric centre. The atmosphere, the beliefs and the patterns of behaviour were completely dominant, ensured by the rule of conformity.

I lasted six months there. While I was there, I was thinking whether I should try to find an alternative school and teach there. Maybe that was the environment I needed, somewhere off the main avenue. There were a few around, but I had some reservations about them. Hadn't I said to myself at the beginning that my career (my destiny) was not in teaching? Moreover, I faced the same barrier as in the Education Department, that I was qualified to teach mathematics, not any other subject. Added to this, funding of alternative schools was poor, and many teachers worked for low pay. I could not afford to go down that road.

I also came across another factor: philosophical warfare. It didn't just happen at university. It seemed to be common that a school would start up in great enthusiasm, get funding together, agree on a curriculum, and start the school. However, after two to five years, two camps would eventuate, and tear the school apart. They would disagree on philosophy and rules, and it would be bitter. I couldn't afford that either. Was it possible for a group of people to avoid such intense squabbles? That seemed to be of overriding importance.

The world is imperfect, but when things become particularly dire, perhaps a new start is necessary. I was thinking about going a long way away, into the country. I was reading magazines about alternative lifestyles. For the moment it was just an idea.

Other things were relevant, too. I was with a woman, and she was expecting a baby. That was wonderful, but life was turbulent, and I was increasingly dissatisfied with work and society. I wanted to get away. As an interim step, I applied for a teaching job in regional Queensland. I thought I would teach there for a while, then we would figure out how we could move into the bush with an alternative community.

This seemed to settle any career questions that might still be lurking. There would be no career. There would be a new life in an alternative community. If fortunate, it would be a beacon to a society that had lost its way. It would show a better way.

It's easy to say now that that was improbable. I am not so cynical. I think something was possible. It's just that it assumes a lot of shared faith and understanding. People fall short. They pull back in moments when extra commitment is required. They get embroiled in money questions when what is required is not very much. But it is hard to break away from social shackles. Perhaps we need to find a middle position, whatever that is.

After a period at a school in Queensland, I spent more than five years extricating myself from society, from a job and a suburban life, to try to create a viable life in the country. But the string was never broken; there was always some kind of bond. One is always a certain number of kilometres from a town, one always has to have some cash, there are always groceries we need to buy, inconsequential though they may be.

I tried. I had a country cottage that was mine. I had a large vegetable garden. I had no ambitions. I was disappointed in the world, but not with life around me. But I never found a self-contained alternative community. You could argue that there was no possibility of a viable, or even identifiable, alternative community.

I had tried to have a goal, an alternative community. What would it have done? Would it have supported me? Or would I have been a leader in it? How would it have fitted into the local environment or the township? I didn't feel capable of being a leader of the community. I lacked charisma. But I also didn't feel there was enough momentum to create this alternative community.

People had come from other places and had brought the same ways with them. They were escaping from something, or they wanted to be something I thought was just a reflection of something I hadn't liked in the city. Just because they were here, it didn't mean they were like-minded. I kept my own company more often. When there were gatherings, I didn't really know what other people were thinking, and I eventually decided it didn't really matter,

Did I still have a goal in life? Something had not worked out, but had I learned anything? Was I just a long way behind where I had been when I was in my early twenties, with some catching up to do?

No, I didn't feel that way. I had learned some things, and I had changed a lot. I was not the same person I was in my early twenties. I had a much better idea of how people can behave, and what it was reasonable to expect from them. With this, I had more confidence in what I could do in groups of people. I also had a better idea of how I wanted to spend my time. I wanted some interaction with people, not just to dig in my garden all day every day. Although, I wanted that too, in some measure.

Would a career plan have helped me now, a new one, a revised one? No, that wasn't what was needed. What made a difference from this point onwards was opportunity. But opportunity is something that you only see if you are primed for it.

When I was living at one house in the country, I was gradually bringing myself around to the idea that I would get a job again. It wouldn't necessarily be teaching, but it could be. We lived near a country town, a long way from any city. It would be different. I was ready to exercise my skills in the classroom again, if need be, and do some small amount of good.

The local paper was delivered with the mail, and I used to read it during the day, in between sessions in my very large garden. This year I had decided to enter some of my vegetables in the local horticultural show. I did, and I won several prizes (the prize being a small certificate that said you had won First, Second or Third prize).

I used to read the whole paper, the articles, the classifieds and the advertisements. It gave me a sense of what happened in the area. There was a Wanted column, and people would say all sorts of things that they wanted, usually farm machinery, but this day one of the advertisements said a Technics Teacher was wanted in a small school. I thought that was bizarre. Why wasn't the advertisement in the Employment column?

Not that I thought I could be a Technics teacher, but I was open-minded, and who else was going to find the advertisement? I rang the school, and went for an interview. I suspect I was the only person who had responded. It was a small Catholic school in a small town not too far away. It was recently formed from separate male and female schools, so they were looking for someone who might be congenial to the new spirit they were trying to develop.

I think I was not too overbearing, and I was academically respectable, and I had had experience in both the city and a regional town. I wasn't Catholic, but nor were most of the staff. I was surprised that they welcomed me, but they did. Despite the fact that I wasn't Catholic, they seemed to respect me, and they seemed to accept that I was competent to teach. It's amazing how much difference that can make to your actual competency!

And I learned how to teach manual arts: woodwork, metalwork and technical drawing. My truncated engineering education satisfied them that I could come to grips with it. My teaching philosophy is that you should be able to pick up any subject up to the end of Year Ten. And in doing so, you can impart that confidence to the children as well. Later on, I taught casually at another high school, and I taught many different subjects. It didn't take the students long to accept that I knew my way around the syllabus.

Among my casual teaching experiences, the most amusing one was when I was offered a sewing class for the day. My mother had been a dressmaker, but that was hardly a qualification for teaching a sewing class. The deputy headmaster didn't expect me to teach, but he thought the pupils would be okay if there was someone in attendance to keep an eye on them.

When I entered the classroom, one of the girls sized up the situation (I had taught mathematics to these girls previously), and asked me if it was okay for her to teach the class. I asked the other girls if that was okay, and they were willing, and the girl taught the class. It was a bit tongue-in-cheek, but it was also a plausibly good sewing lesson. The girl was naturally a play actor, and as well, her last name was Writer. At the end of the class, she asked me if she had done a good job. As far as I could see, she had.

What I said before was: destiny (the uncomfortable word) is about an inner drive. At any particular time, it might express itself in different forms, and it may not be exactly what you thought it was going to be, but what you are doing is at least consistent with that inner drive. At times it might be a stretch, but it will always be consistent with that inner drive.

I spent five years in the Catholic school, and I still remember those years fondly. It meant that later on, when I was doing a Bachelor of Business degree and I needed to do casual teaching in order to earn money, I could do so with confidence and without emotional strain.

In the Catholic school job, I was reconciled to the fact that I had a job again. I was a plausible part of the society I had thought I would reject. Had I simply put myself interminably on the bottom rung of a career ladder? My mother was happy. I was still living in the hills, but at least I wasn't living in the hills as a wild hippie anymore. And I was making use of my education as a teacher.

There was no career path at the school, nor did I have a degree. After I had settled down at the school and I had been there a couple of years, the other teacher who taught technics suggested that I could go back to university and get a teaching degree. I could become properly qualified to teach technics. It was a kind suggestion. However, it stirred me up again. It poked at my inner drive. It reminded me that my tenure at the school was not ever intended to be long-term.

This meant that I had to think about what was next, after having felt comfortable and safe for a while. Who was I? What was my career goal? I knew it would not have helped to have a career plan. If I had, my home in the valley would have been up for elimination. If I was serious about a career, I would have to get out of the valley, even out of the town. I would have to go back to the city and carve my career path there. I had sufficient skills, experience and imagination.

But the home was important. In the intervening years, my wife had left, taking the children with her. She moved a long way away. I guessed that she wanted something I didn't, a life in suburbia. I kept in contact with my children, but I wasn't about to move out of the valley. To her, it was all expendable. I don't think she understood its importance to me.

Career plans have nothing to say about such matters. Life involves entanglements. My view was that if my children came to see me there, in the valley, they would at least understand who I was. (And you could ask, dismissively, what does that mean? But I don't care.)

Chapter 4: Working in the community

But always, there is that inner drive. It persists. And opportunities arise around it. Another advertisement appeared in the local newspaper, for a project officer at a local project for unemployed youth. This was a new initiative in communities around Australia, funded by the Federal Government and run by local, community-based committees. What did I know about being a project officer? I thought, as much as anyone else might.

I had grown in confidence. Was my inner drive taking shape? I thought that a job like this required being able to reconcile two perspectives: what did this job mean at the level of society, and how could one relate to unemployed youth on a day-to-day level? And it helped to be able to articulate this to a selection committee.

What was my goal in the job? Was I a radical? No, I was focused on what I could achieve in the job. The young people needed a job, and they needed skills. Unemployment was obvious in the town, and it led to troubles. The business people, just wanted it to go away (or the young people to go away), although they didn't see any role for themselves in that.

One attitude towards the young people was to amuse them with crafts. The assumption was that over time, things would change. The young people would get a job, or they would go away, and everything would be fine again. The job was seen as simply keeping them off the streets and out of trouble. I wasn't interested in that avenue. I had no judgement to make about it; I just wasn't interested in spending my time doing crafts. I had been a teacher, and I was interested in training.

That wasn't exactly true; I was interested in learning, not training, but it was close enough. The committee liked my approach, so I got the job. Accordingly, I left the Catholic school, having been there five years. Perhaps I was the perfect person for the job: someone who had no career plan but nevertheless still had a strong sense of purpose.

There were some happy times at the centre. When it was functioning smoothly, young people turned up, and were interested in participating in courses and events we ran. And because they were young, they were interested in many aspects of life, all the questions that tumble around unresolved. We had to play a steadying role, calming things down, offering hope, and coaxing those who had become despondent.

It came to grief at one point because a group of young people, together with an older man, wanted to hijack the centre as their hang-out den, taking it over from more purposeful activities. This was allowed to develop into open thuggery, which the committee was not ready to address. I quit, and the committee was subsequently sacked at a public meeting. I came back under a new committee. It was turmoil for a while, and you could say it was ugly, but I was forthright about what I was doing. My vision was steady.

I was beginning to get an understanding of how politics can operate in community groups. I also learned that some people can harbour revenge for a long time, for no healthy reason, just because their plans were thwarted. These lessons were useful in later work contexts.

In this job, I worked with one other person. I was not the manager; we were co-workers. Nor did I have to manage the funds. The dispersal of funds was discussed in conjunction with the committee. Submissions for funding were also the province of the committee.

There was another activity on the side. I took over the running of adult education classes in the town. I had to organise a program of courses, with someone to run each course, a place to hold them, and sort out funds for the classes and teachers. We had to advertise the programs, and this involved a lot of liaison between people and organisations around town. It gathered momentum. More people were interested in enrolling in courses, and more people were interested in running courses.

It became a connection between the new settlers (the hippies) and the existing community in and around the town. For many, it was the first time they had seen and accepted the other group as humans. The adult education courses began to break down barriers. I realised that the value of jobs was not always in the job description.

Had I realised my career goal now? Would this be okay?

No. I still wasn't earning sufficient money, and I didn't have security in my work. I didn't think the job at the unemployment centre would last, and it was a bit discomforting to work for the committee. It was an untrustworthy vehicle. There was the renegade who was not above using thuggery to achieve his goals, and there were professional and business people who had little sympathy with what the centre was doing. Eventually there was another blow-up, and this time I left and did not come back. I stayed home for several months, content to live modestly on unemployment benefits myself.

It doesn't seem to be much of a career plan when you go home and stay there. Had I lost my inner drive? Had I reached the end of the road?

I did wonder, but sometimes you have to be content not to have an answer for a while. It was very beautiful in the valley. I had a garden, I had friends, and no one pressured me about getting a job again. I could have existed like this for a long time.

This time, the job came to me. The employment office had found a job they thought I should apply for. It was as the manager for a community organisation. The organisation had a number of services, but it had not had a manager up until now. It needed someone to coordinate the services and to manage the staff and the funds.

This extended beyond what I had done at the unemployment centre. I had not managed staff and I had not managed funds. I had not made submissions for funds or accounted for money spent. Could I do these things? The employment office apparently thought I could.

I had been thinking, while I was sitting at home. The important thing was that I wanted to stay here. If I was to do that for the longer term, I needed to find a job that paid me properly. I had left teaching, after about ten years in all. That was one goal achieved. But it wouldn't mean much if I didn't find a well-paying job. But a manager? Could I do it?

Yes, I could. I had done the hands-on job of project officer. I had managed the programs for the adult education group. In a small way, I had started to handle money. During the interview process, it became clear to me that this job was the next step. Once again, it wasn't going to be a job for life, but the next step for me was to learn how to do the job of manager. It was being handed to me.

The job was mine. I had the residual thought, "I wonder who else was considered for this job?" but it wasn't critical for me to know. I looked over my history: engineering degree (unfinished), Arts degree (unfinished), teacher with several years' experience, project officer in a youth service, coordinator of adult education programs, and now this. And I had lived in Sydney, Queensland, and now the far north coast of New South Wales.

I was starting to sound well-rounded. During the first week in the job, the chairman of the committee circulated a profile of me to the staff, which gave highlights of my background, and it said that I had both an engineering degree and an Arts degree. I was a trifle uncomfortable about that, because I think truth is important. I did clarify this with the staff when I got the opportunity. I got the feeling they were not surprised at the chairman's leap of fancy.

While I was familiarising myself with the records, I came across a folder which contained details of the applicants for my job. Apart from myself, there was only one other person, and it was the crony from the unemployment centre who had tried to stand over me on behalf of his little mates. So, apparently I was a better candidate than that.

I was clear at this point. I was following my inner drive. I had taken a job which seemed to be a good opportunity, and I was going to learn how to be a manager, with three different services, about six staff, and funding of several hundred thousand dollars. I didn't yet have an office, just a room at the side of a church, but there was the promise of an office soon, and a car.

The chairman made a lot of positive noises. I saw him several times the first week. He wanted to make sure I was settled. His day job was as manager of a building society. He told me to take my time getting to know the files, and to familiarise myself with each of the services: "Take your time."

However, the thing I was most concerned about was the money. I felt that I could master it in time, but I needed to start. There was also the issue that the organisation was in the midst of its annual audit, so the books were still at the accountants. After about a week of this situation, I began to feel that the chairman was holding off on me, and I wondered why. Moreover, I didn't know who I could ask. It was early days. Who could I trust, and who could I talk to without looking like a fool?

It was the weekend, and my unease was increasing. I had begun to think I would have to decide on a plan the next day, something dramatic. Should I front the chairman?

The issue was resolved for me on Sunday night, when I received a phone call at home about nine pm. It was someone from the committee, ringing to tell me that the chairman had been arrested. Tomorrow, I should report to the auditors' offices and it would be explained.

I calmed myself by telling myself that whatever had happened, it was not my fault, and I had done nothing wrong. Did I still have a job? I didn't know, but I had only been there a week, so I would recover.

The chairman, who was also the District Governor of the Apex Club, a young man and quite a local figure, had been arrested after an investigation of several months. He had embezzled all the organisation's money, so much so that he had advised them to take out an overdraft, and then stolen all that money too. Because he was the manager of the local building society, he was able to forge documents claiming that all the money was in various investment accounts. These accounts did not exist.

Needless to say, the people on the committee were stunned and disbelieving. They had trusted this man. The auditors also were devastated, although they should not have trusted the documents he produced for them. There was culpability there, and they knew it.

But my concern was the staff and the services. I had already slipped into warrior mode, and I was responsible for defending them. Later on, I realised that I needn't have taken this stance. I could have decided, "Oh well, that job didn't work out", and just walked off. I didn't even think to do that. I was immediately thinking about the funding bodies and the local politicians, and about talking to them. Our organisation had a central body in Sydney, and I talked to them about what we could do to ensure short-term funds to pay staff and keep services afloat.

There was action. The Federal Government and State Government both came aboard with funds. There was talk about our longer-term plans. I was thrust fairly quickly into planning mode. I had done this in a modest way with the adult education group, and I had to rapidly step up to learn what would be appropriate and feasible in my current context. I established connections with the Federal and State local members of parliament, and with staff in the relevant government departments.

What might have been a slow, unwieldy introduction to the job turned into what they call a baptism of fire. The criminal case for the chairman featured in the local newspapers, which meant that our organisation did too, and I had to make the most of that.

At the same time, there are issues of philosophy that sit in the background unexamined until the light shines on them. I had come out of teaching, radical social thinking, and the functioning of community groups. I thought there was something productive we could be doing, given the chance. I was also discovering that it helps to be articulate. One should hold back from being crazy, but one should establish a firm basis for adventurous plans.

Eventually, over six years, I built a plant nursery in which most of the adult clients in the service could work, and it started to establish a viable market in the local region. But my path led out of there. I became competent at all the things that managers do. I managed staff, I guided programs for clients, I looked after the finances. We started with an exercise book, and graduated to a commercial accounting program. We were a model for other services, both in administration and in the work that we did with clients.

I remained naive in the sense that I did not realise that when you are successful, people will swarm around. You think they are supportive, but they are trying to get a piece of the action for themselves, either dishonestly or obsequiously. Before I knew it, I was snared, and accused of dishonesty and incompetence.

It was especially galling because of the criminal situation I had faced at the end of the first week on the job. At one point it was even inferred that I was complicit in that criminality, which was impossible because I hadn't even been there at the time. I found this staggering, so I didn't know how to combat it. It was a disgusting set of circumstances.

I think I would deal with things differently now, but although I fought bravely then, I was defeated. I was sacked and maligned. I was smeared in the local paper deliberately, by people who were part of the ugliness. I went home again and I stayed there. There were some small skirmishes where I could take a stand, but the damage had been done. I had no job and now, and no one who would give me a job.

You call that a career plan? The only niggle in all this was that I remembered back to when I started. I had told myself, you are not a manager, just as you are not a teacher. You are here to learn how to be a manager. It is important, it is part of your future. But you should reconsider it after five years. By then, you should have learned what you need to know.

And all the trouble had happened in year six. And yes, I did think of it at the end of year five. But you know what it's like.... I had built the services up fivefold in five years: the number of clients we served, the budget, the number of staff and, I told myself, things still need to be consolidated, and who else would step into my shoes? They were compelling reasons, so I pressed on.

Further, I had no idea why knowing how to be a manager was important. I had enjoyed being a manager, with the whole range of tasks and challenges it involved. If I had one word to use for being a manager, it would be "integration". One should be abreast of the whole range of tasks involved in a project or organisation, from the philosophy of what you are doing through to the practicalities, the logistics, the finances, the communication, and the relationships between people. You need to know how to weave it all together cohesively.

I suppose, at the broadest level, my inner drive was to understand things and articulate them. That's very broad, but there were contexts where I was interested in applying these goals. After I got over my hurt, I was sure that would become apparent.

As ever, I always started with the practical goal: how are you going to sustain yourself and your family? In the country, one can live on the dole for a while, which gives you some sense of the latitude available to you, but one knows that after a while things will become lean. At least it gave me some thinking time.

I could have fought to get my job back. It was suggested to me. But I thought that would be crazy. There would still be people around me who were trying to break me, for whatever reasons. So, I declined. I think part of my reasons were that I had broken my own vow. But I didn't say that to anyone; that was my own personal business.

I would walk down the street in town and people would be quiet. I didn't know what they were thinking. I had lived in this town peaceably and honestly for over ten years. All I could do was stand up straight. I was not guilty of anything wrong. Others were.

How do ordinary folk react when they read a story on the front page of their local paper, written by the paper's main journalist, about you, implying your guilt? I did take action through the Press Council. I got a weak retraction six weeks later in a small paragraph on page six. The filth was winning.

After months of living quietly, I figured something out. I would go to university. I doubted that I would get another job in the area, and what sort of job would I do anyway? I had held a prominent position in the community. There wasn't exactly anywhere else to jump to.

Going to university was a step sideways. It was a good plan. I had been to university twice, and bailed out each time after about two years. They were not failures; I had ensured that much.

Moreover, I still wasn't interested in completing either of those two degrees. The engineering course had served to get me into teachers' college, and it had helped to get me the job at the Catholic school. The Arts units had been added to my teaching qualification. The nice thing about this was that if I wanted to, I could continue to teach without having to go back to university to complete a university degree in teaching. That would have been a legacy of my original fast track into teaching.

I had, in recent years, rejected the idea of going to university to obtain a degree relevant to technics teaching. So, what was my interest now? After all the turmoil, I had not been reduced to accepting that my fate in life was to be a teacher. It was that inner drive again: No! My fate was not to be a teacher! It was something else, that would align with that inner drive that I still could not articulate.

This thinking was also in defiance of another clear possibility: I had proved myself as a manager. I could leave the valley, go somewhere else and get another job as a manager. I had to consider the possibility, and not be obstinate. I did consider the idea. But, I rejected it. I wasn't ready to leave this home of mine. I had been through many trials there, but through all of that, it was my home. In all of my life, this was the place I called home. I remembered, when I was twenty-seven, "coming home to a place he'd never been before".

So, university. What was I intending to do there? Not teaching? No, not teaching. Teaching had stalked me since I was a child. It was not a bad thing, but it was not the end goal, not for me. I kept thinking about why I had had the job as the manager for the last six years. Obviously, I was marked out for it. I had never been a manager, and somebody in authority contacted me and asked me to apply for the job. There was no one else in competition for the role. Then, after one week, there was a disaster. The chairman had been arrested, and I discovered that all the money had been taken. (After his arrest, he was found guilty and he went to gaol, but most of the money had been squandered or spirited away.)

From these ashes, I had made a success of the job. I built up services that enabled people to live as best they could, with appropriate support. I established a viable business and provided employment for people. It was a model for other services. I could easily have seen all this as a platform for other endeavours. I could have replicated and extended what I had done here somewhere else.

However, my inner drive wasn't saying that. I had reined myself in, and I was asking myself, what had been the greater goal, if the point of that job was just to learn how to be a manager, to gain a deep, practical understanding of all the challenges of the managerial role? I didn't know, but the next step was to go to university to study management. I enrolled in a Bachelor of Business degree. Perhaps, after twenty-five years, I would actually obtain a degree.

There was a side issue here. My managerial experience covered the best part of ten years. I could easily have talked my way into a Masters degree, a Master of Business Administration (MBA). But I didn't want to do that. I was looking back at two unfinished Bachelor degrees and thinking, this time, I will finish a Bachelor degree, in my chosen area. I thought that it would be great fun to be doing this backwards. I had been a manager for ten years, and now I would learn how to do it!

And it was so. Every subject we did in the degree, I had a context for. I had personal experience that lifted the subject out of textbook theory. So often I found myself saying, "So that's what I was doing all those years!" I finally had the theory that made sense of all the things I had done intuitively. And I was interested in the theory.

Chapter 5: Back to university

At this stage I was in my forties. It could be argued that I was simply avoiding work, or rather, I was avoiding making a choice about what work to do. I had had a well-paid job. I could easily have found myself another well-paid job. I might have had to move, but many people do that in order to build a career. It wasn't too late for me. But here I was, it could be said, hiding out in the country. It wasn't beneficial to myself or anyone else.

"They will say you are like a gong that has not been struck. You have not yet shown what you are, or what you can do."

I could also say, aren't I hopelessly unqualified to be talking about career goals or career plans?

And yet, there had been moments. I was sitting in my house out in the country, just tending my garden, and a paper was thrown over the fence. When I read it, there was the most unexpected job in it for me. Would I seriously have thought to apply for a job as a Technics teacher at a Catholic school? Yet I spent five good years there, playing a worthwhile role in a new, growing school community.

My more recent experience had been a deep learning experience. I had learned the wide range of skills and experiences that the managerial role entails. It was part of me now. And it had been far better than being an underling in a big company, because I was responsible for everything. If I didn't know how to do something, I had to learn it. I had had to learn personal qualities too. I knew that there were some activities I was more comfortable with than others, so I had to make sure I kept a balance, and made enough time for the more difficult things too.

I had had to develop and extend myself. I knew that none of this would be contained in a degree, but I knew it was also necessary. A degree would just be "book learning", but a degree would also be a weapon and armour. There had been critics at the organisation who said I was just a burnt-out schoolteacher, implying I didn't really know how to manage the organisation.

It was vicious nonsense. For a start, I was not a burnt-out schoolteacher. I had an excellent teaching record. I simply wasn't teaching anymore. And I hadn't failed as a manager. My achievements were solid and obvious. But it could be argued that I didn't have a qualification to be a manager. Mind you, nor did most people working as managers in the same sector.

But a side benefit of having a degree would be that such people would have to shut up. However, this was not why I was doing the degree. I was doing the degree for delight. After the troubles of the last couple of years, it was something I could plunge into with enthusiasm. In fact, I could plunge into it with the enthusiasm of someone who had not fulfilled himself as a student in the past twenty-five years.

In fact, my last scholastic achievement was at the end of high school, when I was the Dux of the school. All the choices I made when I was around twenty were driven by practicality: the need to get into the workforce as soon as possible, and not be dependent on my mother. I had charted my way from there, to Queensland, to the bush, in response to that inner drive. Did going to university this time mean I was starting over, as if for the first time, and this time I would be successful?

There was one other element of my plan. I had a family and I needed to work as well as study in order to keep the household afloat. I would apply to do casual teaching. Finally, I had the right mindset to do it without drama or emotional struggle. I would only work at the high school in my own town. That way I would get to know the other teachers and all the pupils. When a casual teacher arrives in a school and they are not known, there are always children who will test them out. They will push and push to get a reaction, and that happens constantly. I had done it before, and it was tedious.

I went to the local high school and made myself known. I thought, just going to one school I wouldn't get much work, especially because teachers are generally identified as the teacher of one subject. However, I let it be known that I could teach mathematics through to Year 12, and Technics, but I was willing to teach most other subjects to year 10. This meant that the other teachers of those subjects at the school had to be confident about me as well, or they would block me.

Gradually I gained acceptance, among both teachers and students, so I got a steady stream of work during the four years I spent at university. Sometimes it was a bit too much. I was notionally full-time at university, but sometimes I was teaching three days a week. I had to capitalise on my strong understanding of the material in the university subjects and work my way through it quickly.

Writing essays was a good practice. I had consciously developed my writing skills in the management job. There are many writing tasks in the managerial role, but many managers do not like writing, so they do it in a rudimentary way. I did it well. I also wrote and issued a regular newsletter to all the families of the services. It was a professional piece of work that I was pleased with. It cemented our standing in the community too. I wrote submissions for funding, setting out the purpose for the funds, and the process by which we would bring the projects to fruition. We were very successful in obtaining funds. It helps to be articulate.

One aspect of this writing that was important to me was honesty. Our submissions were solid because they were all based on the truth. I did not make up lies to bolster our case, and I knew that everything we claimed we could demonstrate if need be. Occasionally there would be someone on the committee who would suggest putting a shinier spin on our claims, but I resisted. Always know you are standing on solid ground.

Did I have reservations about going back to teaching? Did I fear being sucked back into the great machine? When I was in the manager's job, at one point, one of the committee members made a snide offer to me. He insinuated that if I could be seen to be amenable, they would get me a bigger car. When I had been given a car, I deliberately chose one that was modest. It served my purposes well enough, and in a small community, I did not want to be seen as ostentatious or self-important. He obviously didn't understand this, because he was offering me something that was the opposite, and it would destroy my relationship with the local people.

The point was, the man said to me, "We own you. We own your whole life. You depend on us, and we can make things sweet for you."

I thought he was joking, but I could quickly see that he wasn't. There was a nasty undertone to it. He was purporting to threaten me. Very quickly, I said to him, "You don't own me at all. You rent me for forty hours a week." I made it hard, and I didn't embellish. I let it hang in the air. You might begin to understand why I got the sack a few months later. But what I said was true: they didn't own me, in any sense of the word.

Nor did the school or the education department. I was happy to give of myself, but I was working there for a purpose, to earn my way through university. One has to free oneself of the idea that one is dependent. This can be a conundrum, but it is important to resolve it.

One cannot hope to pursue a career plan until one has addressed this question.

And still I did not know what the future would be, and I was in my forties. I could not see that a Bachelor of Business degree would propel me into high school teaching. Business Studies was now taught in school, but there was a great mismatch between doing a business degree and teaching elementary economics to teenagers.

But I did write good essays. I majored in human resource (HR) management, and we did one unit in Equal Opportunity. For my essay, I wrote about equal opportunity in pay and conditions for female teachers in New South Wales. The lecturer said I should submit it to a journal. I didn't, I was not ready to step up to that, but it was gratifying to be told that.

I did the essay because when I was a young teacher, the memory of the restrictions on pay and conditions for women was still fresh. At one point, female teachers were expected to resign when they got married. And their pay rate was maybe 70 percent of the male rate of pay. Today that seems ridiculously improper. The difference then was that many male teachers had lived their whole lives in that environment, so it was easy for them to think that it was okay.

In three years, I completed my Bachelor of Business degree. Most of the other students were young, in their early twenties. The university was new; it had been a teachers' college and the Federal Government wanted to set up a network of regional universities. That was fine, it served my purposes, but I never thought it was my destination (or destiny). But I was getting closer to the time when I would have to think about what I was going to do next. What was my next job going to be? Not teaching? Not a job at university? Not a manager of an organisation?

Note that the idea of being a writer did not occur to me. Nor was there any reason why it should. A job being a writer was just as unavailable then as it had ever been. The only people who make a living as a writer are novelists who sell a million books every time they release a novel. Of course, they are other kinds of people you could name as well, but it would just underline the point.

I realised that I had a viable lifestyle for the time being. I was getting enough work as a casual teacher, and I could manage the work and study requirements. I could do the Honours year. I had won a prize when I completed the Bachelor degree, for being the best student in the Human Resource Management stream. Perhaps this augured well. It would take one year to complete the Honours part.

Doing the Honours year would mean having to write an Honours thesis. What would I do? Did I have anything in mind? While I was studying, I had been mulling over my performance as a manager. Had it been satisfactory? Could I have done anything better? I felt that I had done the best I could, and had I done it all in reverse, with the degree before the experience, I don't think I could have done much better. The dominant theme was the dishonesty and viciousness of a group of people. Why didn't I examine that in my Honours thesis?

I could have examined the structures involved, or communication. I chose to examine the topic of ethics. I didn't base it in a small organisation. I decided to examine human resource managers and their understanding of ethics in their role. My idea was that ethics is probably not a big deal most of the time. Most organisations are probably reasonably ethical, or at least law-abiding. But how would human resource managers react if they were faced with unethical conduct in the organisation? Were they clear enough about ethical values that they would know straight away what was acceptable and what was not, and how to go about addressing it?

It seemed like a good-enough idea, and my supervisor, who had faced ethical issues himself during his career (and probably many people have), was sympathetic. I devised a plan for pursuing my thesis, and methods of addressing the questions. I got in contact with the national institute for human resource management and asked them for access to their members. My supervisor was helpful, and organised for the two of us to speak at a human resources conference on a topic concerning ethics and HR. So, I gained some experience of speaking at conferences too.

Was that part of my career plan, given that I didn't think I would end up working at a university?

The thesis was a sizeable piece of work, something I had not needed to tackle before, but I proved to be competent at it. Its scope was appropriate to the Honours level, although I also felt it would have served as a Masters thesis, given the several theses that I looked at. The two examiners were satisfied with it.

I was rewarded with an honour, the University Medal. I was told about it a week before the ceremony. My supervisor was very pleased. He thought I deserved it. For a regional city, the university's awards ceremony was a big event, and among the many photos of the ceremony, there was mine with the medal and my certificate of Bachelor of Business with First Class Honours, featured in the local newspaper.

It put a seal on the events of years ago. Here was the sacked manager proving that he had a thorough understanding of the management role, and conducting an inquiry into ethics and management. I was satisfied with what I done to reorient my life since the disaster.

It still didn't resolve what I was going to do now. Time passes; I was in my late forties. Many people have given up by then and found a moribund job that has a regular pay day. I was living in the country, at a place that I loved, but with no job prospects. And I had a fresh Bachelor of Business degree with First Class Honours.

I had lived in my house for nearly twenty years. I began to think, maybe I should give it up. It's been good, but I hold it within. Since I moved into this house, I have done so many things, and I should recognise that they may be leading to some goal. The last few years have been stable, like a road going in a particular direction, going somewhere. Maybe I should look outwards. I hold the valley in my heart. It will always be home.

That was a big step. The shift in my thinking did not take place overnight. It took place over months. I kept coming back to the thought: "I hold the valley in my heart. It will always be home. It is time to look outwards."

After I finished at university, I continued to teach at the high school. I knew some teachers who had been doing this for years. It was their way of life. But not mine. There was no offer of tutoring at the university. But then I found a part-time job in Brisbane at a university as a tutor in Business Ethics. That was almost too good to be true. It was two days a week. It was problematic, because it took three hours to drive to Brisbane, and then three hours home afterwards.

But it was a step in the right direction. I felt I would be okay at university if I was teaching business ethics. Otherwise, human resource management would be fine. Most importantly, I was looking outside of my home town. I was opening the doors.

Over the next few months, I applied for more than a hundred jobs in distant cities and towns. I would have to move. None of the jobs were in my own region; the jobs there were few. But that was okay. I had already made my decision.

Then there was a close call. There was the dream job. It was at a regional university (a few hours from my home), working at a university for a professor, lecturing, but also working on a large national study that was about the effects of downsizing. At the end of three years, you would receive a PhD. It was perfect. It was a paid job, combined with research for the professor, and at the end of the study, you would receive a PhD.

The professor knew he was carrying a golden gift, an unbelievable prize, and he wanted the best students/researchers to work for him. He seemed to think I would fit. I even had teaching experience, as well as my new Honours degree. But I responded to him in dismay. I said, if I do a PhD, I want it to be my work, not someone else's. This is not what I wanted. He, in turn, was dismayed. He stated the obvious, that this job was a rare opportunity.

I said I would think it over, but I didn't. Yes, it was a rare opportunity, but I couldn't do it. It was back to that inner drive. This job was a prize for someone else, someone who clearly wanted to be a lecturer at university. I wasn't even sure about that. Did I really know what I wanted to do, still?

I went home and went back to the newspapers, looking up the Employment columns. At this stage I had been for a dozen job interviews, travelling to a city each time. Mostly it was fairly clear quite early that, as they say these days, "we were not a good fit". That expression is a camouflage for anything a company wants it to be. It has nothing to do with understanding or competency to do the job.

There was one interview which was for a public service job in HR, and there was a panel of about six people, so it was very unwieldy. All of the people were struggling for relevance. It was only the second question asked, and I gave what I thought was a proper answer, and one that was in line with my values. I could tell immediately that the man who asked the question took a dislike to me.

I realised that he was important, and that that was the end of my job prospects here, so I took his reaction as incitement. My answer had been appropriate, and I wouldn't have changed it at all, so I simply toyed with the rest of the questions, puzzling some of the interviewers, and offending a few of them. No loss; it would not have been a congenial place to work.

In some cases, I thought that I was disregarded because I lived a long way away. Fair enough, I suppose they thought that if I was serious about a job, I would already live nearby. But some organisations tried to be fair.

In one instance, I got an interview for a job in Sydney, but I happened to be in Brisbane that day, tutoring in Business Ethics. They tried to accommodate me by providing for me to do a telephone interview. But this was in the days before mobile phones, and I had to do the interview from a public phone, keeping an eye on the coins and the credit while I was talking. It was rather hopeless. They also let me know how many people they were interviewing: ten. From an interviewer's perspective, I think it is very difficult to make judgements between ten people. One should try to trim the list a bit more before that stage.

That job was for an adult education coordinator's job. It was much bigger than what I had done, but I could have done it. Did I want to? I did need a job, or I would be casual teaching forever.

And then, in a Saturday newspaper, there was an advertisement for a writer. It was a publishing company, and they were looking for somebody to write about human resources for a professional audience. I immediately thought, "I don't want a job working in human resources, I want a job writing about human resources!"

There was the same problem, that I lived in a little valley in the country, a very long way away from the relevant city. I wondered if they would be fair to me. I understood all the reasons why they wouldn't be. It was a private company; they were not under the same obligations to be fair (in practice) as a government department was. But by this time, I had refined my curriculum vitae and it was, I think, impressive. And my argument was that I had both the academic grounding and many years of practical experience in business. I could articulate all aspects of the human resources role. I had a good understanding of law from my Business degree and, it never hurt that I had been a teacher.

They replied to me, and we had a telephone conversation, which was encouraging. They asked me if I was serious about coming to the city. And they asked me to write a piece, which would be a summary of a government report on the education of managers. They posted it to me, I wrote the piece, and mailed it back to them. Everyone waited for the mail to play its part. Life is so different now.

They asked me again if I was serious about coming to the city to take up the job. I assured them that I was very ready, and I would be excited to take up the job. This was what I wanted to do. I felt that there was some appreciation of my perspective, and that they would honour the agreement. I had to ask them for a favour, too. I said I was leaving my home in the country after twenty years, and I had to prepare everything for that eventuality, so could I have six weeks before I started work? It was a big thing to ask, but if this was truly my job, they would grant me that favour. And they did.

It was a very packed six weeks. I had to find some renters to move into my house, I had to find a place to rent in the city, I had to organise removalists and I had to coordinate it all. I had to communicate with all manner of people, having suddenly decided to move out of the community after twenty years.

It all happened in due course, and I began work as a writer at a publishing company in the city, something that other people did in their twenties. I was in my late forties. But it didn't matter. I belonged there, and I would prove my competence. I would do good things.

Chapter 6: The real apprenticeship

I felt as if this period of time was my real apprenticeship. It was my apprenticeship as a writer, in my case, writing commentary and articles for HR professionals. I had to produce material every day, so I had to quickly become accomplished at the process: planning articles, gathering or preparing the appropriate materials, including law-based content, structuring articles for a professional audience, and editing. I had to become assured and independent at this, so that I could take charge of particular publications.

I had to have a sense of the whole of a publication, which could be a newsletter of a few pages, but up to a solid, comprehensive reporter of three thousand pages. All these publications had been devised years ago, so a group of people had created the structure and content. But the environment continually changed, and the material had to remain relevant, so occasionally it had to be restructured. We had to keep abreast of the law in a given area, and of industry trends, as well as the rhetoric of the field, so we were seen to remain relevant.

Gradually I gained in confidence and could see where imperfections existed in publications. I made small forays into amending commentary. Over time, I could take on a topic and make extensive changes to it. There were enough existing models of commentary for me to follow. We were given enough latitude to attend seminars and conferences, so that we could keep subscribers up to date. I established a pattern of work so that I could meet my deadlines reliably.

It wasn't long before I had a great deal of autonomy, and my work was trusted. For now, this work was a clear expression of inner drive. This was what I felt I was meant to be doing. There were some aspects that were irksome, such as having to write reports for a payroll manual, but it was also gratifying to be competent at that. It was also at the time when the internet swept through the workplace and made many aspects of our work more seamless. It wasn't uniformly so, but the trend was in that direction.

Was this the end of the story? No. There were new issues. One was about working with others. I was able to develop my own ideas about what needed to happen next in the development of the work, but often, our managers did not share that clarity. They were focused on cutting costs and quick returns in profits, and had little interest in the commentary itself. They had all been educated in the school that thought you didn't need to know anything about the content of a filed in order to manage processes in that field.

I was working for a publishing company in the commercial sphere that was one of the biggest in the world, and which always had a firm eye on profit. That was fine in itself, but how would I fare in this environment? Would it give me enough room to breathe? I knew that my work was competent. Would that be enough for me to survive? Or would I find myself expendable?

Another consideration was whether I should aim at becoming a manager in this place. I had years of management experience which included budget oversight and service development. I could see how I would be useful in a management role here. A couple of times, there were opportunities to apply for a management role, but I was rejected. I was clearly more qualified than the people who were given the positions. I thought that it must be because the company did not want to lose me as a writer.

I asked for more money and was given a little, something to keep me mollified. But there was a question of what my career plan was now. How long did I expect to be doing this job, or this work? There were some people around my age in the company who had settled down for the long haul. They read the job down to its minimal, moribund level, which was possible. There were younger people who had already moved on, for a variety of reasons. What were my plans?

I thought that online learning was burgeoning as the online environment was growing, so I would like to move into that field, and combine my knowledge of teaching with my knowledge of management and employment law. The company offered a study package; they would pay for employees to do a higher degree as long as you continued to work for them for twelve months following your completion of the degree.

There were universities that offered online study for a Masters degree in online education. That made it possible for me to complete it without having to travel to lectures. It also meant that my current status as a three-year trained teacher would be upgraded, should I ever want to return to teaching. Even if I didn't, there was poetry in the endeavour. It was an upward trajectory from something that began when I was twenty.

It would take me from two to three years to complete the Masters degree. That was fine. However, it was still the early days of the internet, and it was essentially a correspondence course. There was an online discussion group, but it seemed peripheral to the main work. There were lots of readings, which I printed out on the printers at work. There were a couple of units where there were minor tests, but the primary form of assessment was through assignments. I had checked that out beforehand; I was not interested in examinations. That was an adolescent modality.

There were eight units. Some of them used the vocabulary of instructional design, so afterwards I could say I was an Instructional Designer, and I actually could design courses of instruction in a variety of topics for online environments. Towards the end of my course of study, my company began to establish a group for online training. Companies were quick to see that online compliance training would be a huge benefit to them over face-to-face training, and my company was quick to see that it had the knowledge base to produce suitable courses and even to administer them.

Naturally I thought that the company would include me in this new venture. I was encouraged, because the online learning group made use of me to write some courses in equal employment opportunity, and work health and safety. They were using an external online design company, so I could keep my focus on the content rather than on the technicalities. Around the time that I finished my degree, a Master of Education in Online Education, with Distinctions or High Distinctions in all units, a position was advertised in this group, and I applied.

I had all the requirements of the job description, strong field knowledge, and I was already part of the company. I doubted whether there was anyone else around who fitted the bill. And I wasn't given the position. It went to someone who was far less qualified. I wondered why. I enquired, and it was obvious that my movement had been blocked, because the manager of my current team did not want to lose a good writer.

It was bizarre that they had allowed me to study for the qualification that it was not going to allow me to pursue. I simmered over that for a while, flattering though it was to be appreciated in my current role. And yes, there was pleasure in being competent at a job.

The inner drive is always there, even if it lurks beneath the surface for periods of time. What was it telling me now? And yes, one voice was reminding me, you don't have to do anything. You can do what other people are doing, which is to reduce the job to its minimal level and relax. Get a hobby. You could even decide to write poetry, and copy the poems into an exercise book.

On the other hand, did I feel that I had fulfilled my destiny? I remembered the words: "Live long enough to fulfil your destiny." Conversely, I knew I should not allow myself to slip into the hands of fate.

Had I fulfilled my destiny? Or, in contemporary terms, had I fulfilled my potential and used my skills to do something worthwhile in the world that only I could do?

No. I could accept that I might be moving towards it, perhaps still in a haphazard way, but still towards it, but I could not say that I had fulfilled it. Not at all. It had not yet even become clear.

The Masters degree had been appropriate, even if it had not eventuated in the position I thought it would lead to. I still had the opportunity in my present role of writing about online learning, as one of the publications that I did the writing for was on training and development. It was a 1,600-page reference manual for training departments. Online learning was an important new area.

I had read something else about destiny. Life is constantly breathing in and out, and our destiny is constantly changing. It is not a fixed thing like a town down the road. Accordingly, we can attune ourselves to it and move with it, or we can be anxious and restless, and unknowingly move against it. The sense of destiny itself can be our biggest problem. Our anxiety and restlessness can be the barrier to our progress.

The usual sentiment in our society is that if you haven't succeeded, you should try harder. It's a subtle thing to think you should be calmer instead. And we need to accept where we are at the moment. Mostly we can only see as far as the next step.

The change I did make at the publishing company, after thinking about it for twelve months, was to change my status. I thought that I might be able to switch from being an employee to being a writer on contract. There were a few other people who had this kind of arrangement. Then I could work from home, and I would not be subject to the day-to-day pressure of being an employee. My work would be defined, and I was quite happy to be responsible for it.

I suppose the time was right for such a move, because no obstacles were put in my way. We agreed on what publications I would be responsible for and what the payment would be. Again, I went home, but this time I took my work with me. I was out of the office politics. The advance of the internet meant that I was able to complete all my work from home. It also meant that if I could organise my time appropriately, I could take up other work.

I loved working from home. I had an office separate from the house, which was of huge importance. It meant that I left the house each morning to go to work, yet I did not have to travel. I caught up with my work colleagues periodically, so I did not feel isolated. Other work came to me, writing articles for other publications, and writing training courses.

I took over the editing of a textbook that my company produced for human resource managers. That meant organising and liaising with around thirty people to write various sections of the book. I wrote some parts myself as well. I thought it was a creditable achievement, and it was a successful endeavour for the company.

Was I there yet? Had I arrived at my goal? Did I have a solid, reliable income? Did I have standing in the community?

It was a bit more like piecing a jigsaw together. For a few years, I edited a magazine for a national membership organisation of trainers. That was a piece of the puzzle. I enjoyed the work, but it wasn't paid well, and it was treated by others in the organisation as a marginal kind of job. I think I lifted the standard of the publication, but I don't think that was appreciated. And indeed, when I left, it quickly reverted back to its scrappy former self.

I did that job in parallel with a number of other contracts. I was still working for the publishing company, although the work was tapering off. I think the advent of the internet negatively affected the areas I was involved in. One year, I worked for a government department creating an online learning course. It had its problems, but I managed to pursue it to a suitable end.

Another year, I worked with another person on creating a training course for coaching, and then another on mentoring. These projects could both be called successful. They were coherent, knowledgeable, and well-packaged. However, I think they would have been more successful for someone whose speciality was training delivery. It was not the writers of the training courses who attracted the money, but those who delivered the courses. Moreover, those who delivered the courses generally did not place much store in the process of writing.

In this environment, it seemed that I was a bit too precious about the quality of the writing, or even the quality of the materials used. Something that was put together much more quickly would suffice.

Another opportunity emerged. I was referred to a tertiary college that offered a Bachelor degree in human resource management, and their delivery mode was online. Was I interested?

I think that part of the reason I was interested was because it was a part-time offering. It didn't mean that I was making a full commitment to this as a career choice. I was being offered one semester, and there may or may not be any more to it that that. And, of course, I hadn't done it before, so it would be interesting and it would extend my skills. I had told myself that I wasn't a teacher, but this was teaching in a new context.

I hadn't taught human resource management before. I had written about it for several years now, so I was an appropriate person to teach it. Perhaps that was enough. If one had the knowledge, one should be prepared to offer it to others. I was satisfied with my reasoning for accepting the role. To be an online lecturer in this subject was not like breaking a vow I had made to myself. It just meant that this was not the endpoint of my career.

I liked the thought that our destiny – our calling, our career – is constantly changing, along with us. You could even say that we and our destiny are constantly tuning into each other. One experience adds something and then we move on. Another experience adds something different.

Each experience is also something in itself. I wasn't taking up lecturing in HR just for the experience. I was also wanting it to be an enjoyable experience in itself. And it was. Most of the students were around the thirty-year mark, not just out of school. Most of them were working, so they had current experience of HR issues to reflect on; it wasn't just textbook learning for them. So, we had some interesting discussions, and their essays were creditable. I even enjoyed marking essays.

I did learn new skills. We had online discussions, both live chat and written discussion boards. And I learn to mark on the computer, using purpose-made software. I did this work for about three years, so I taught a number of subjects: HR topics, employment law, leadership, organisational development. They were all topics I had experienced as a manager, and all subjects I had written extensively about.

After three years, the college finished a cohort of students and they had decided not to continue this degree. The college was part of the business world, and education for it was part of a business plan, with its own priorities and profit that had nothing to do with education. My services were discontinued.

I was not unhappy about this outcome. This work was, again, part of my learning, not part of my ultimate career plan. I mean this jocularly; you would have gathered that I had no career plan.

However, there was discrimination at work. I was always making choices. I had come across the image of a pear seed, and how it grows into a pear tree. It does not grow into a coconut tree. It could, however, grow into a very particular form of pear tree, quite unlike one in the next field. Just so, I would always do things that were consistent with being a pear tree, and I would not do things that were more appropriate to a coconut tree. There was discrimination at work, even if at times it might be hard to see that.

Being an online lecturer in HR was consistent with being a pear tree, and it deepened the skills and knowledge I needed to be a mature pear tree.

All this time, I had continued writing on HR, employment law and training for the publishing company. Across a period of several years, I had changed a great deal through my work outside the company. I had had many different experiences. This would not have happened if I had remained an employee. I had grown many new branches (but I was still a pear tree).

Now the publishing company was also examining its profit and loss, and my area was not a big money-spinner. Most of its profit was in taxation law, accounting, business law, and work health and safety. It was shaving areas off the scope of its publications, and the areas on which I wrote were shaved.

It was sad, because I had kept several publications in good shape. I felt they had been worth the money that they cost customers. They were up to date, they were accurate, and they were relevant and comprehensive. But that's as it should be. I had never been trying to minimise my work. And I was trusted to do a good job. That was who I was.

One can talk about career planning, but at the centre of it should be a commitment to doing good work, and doing decent work for decent pay. This can be a vexatious area. When profit is the primary concern, the workplace can become acrimonious: they don't work hard enough, they don't pay us enough, etc. It can be delicate to find that balance between the parties where the needs are settled and trust can prevail.

And sometimes the pear tree has to find new soil.

My work for the publishing company had been a stable in my life for many years, both financially and in terms of the work itself. I was a writer. Here was a job that validated that conviction constantly, and I could see my work in print, serving its purpose for an audience.

There is a place near the beginning when writing is scary. You write something and then you see it in print. It is done. If it is unsatisfactory or in some way wrong, you stand condemned by your own hand. Others will see that, and the discerning will know it.

I had mastered the work of writing. I knew these risks and knew how to not become a perpetrator of poor work. There is an aspirational part of writing too. One writes to affect readers in some way. Much of my writing was to explain a topic clearly and succinctly. I was also trying to engender values, not values I was trying to impose on people, but values I felt we should all share. Our society relied on these values: truth, competence, fairness. If the writer did not know this, however, he/she could create an environment where people thought it was alright to try and slide around them.

One has to have that clarity of thought. This is where the writing comes from.

What did I do? I needed to find some more work. I had some work, but I needed some more, and I needed the money, too. My roundabout career was respectful of my inner drive, but I also had to respect the impending needs of my retirement years. Not that I was committed to the concept of retirement, but I was destined to age, and I had to be mindful of declining capacities and energy levels.

If one is doing things that one enjoys and gets satisfaction from, the need to retire is not so pressing. This is especially so if one is doing things that only one can do.

One qualification to this truth is that one must be ever mindful of self-delusion. I have seen older people who think they are irreplaceable, but everyone around them does not share their opinion, and it is most uncomfortable. One does not want to be a person like that. To remain sufficiently self-questioning is an important life skill. Most of the skills that are important to career planning are not really job skills; they are life skills.

So, I needed work, having been out of circulation for some time. Bearing in mind that a pear tree should look for a situation that is appropriate to a pear tree, I considered what was salient in my skills and knowledge, and where it would be good to move towards.

I wanted to do more work in creating training programs for the online environment. It would bring together teaching skills, in particular, the design of training courses, along with writing skills, and presumably, subject-matter knowledge.

Later that week, while I worked on a continuing project at home, I received a phone call from someone I had known a couple of years ago in training circles. He asked me if I knew anyone who might be interested in a job designing training programs for professional staff at a university.

I had not previously worked at a university, except for the brief stint as a tutor in Business Ethics. Apart from this, I had come close on occasion, but our paths had not crossed as yet. But this time, I was offered the job and I took it. I had some reservations about the university environment, but if it became too difficult, I could simply leave. I was to be in a staff training unit, not a lecturer working alongside other academics. There might be difficulties that could be ego problems, but I had my own foundation of competency that I could stand on, and I did not need to be apologetic or subservient to anybody.

I had a colleague who was supportive, and there was ample scope for us to build the online capacities of staff training. It was the right time for that to happen. We knew that we could create online programs that would be well-received. We were offering courses that were above the standard that had been previously available, both in quality of content and quality of methodology. I was making use of the knowledge that I had gained while working for the publishing company, and in my Masters degree. And we were given the opportunity to acquire new software, which we learned how to use well.

Despite the successes we attained, there were some entrenched problems. My position was temporary, which meant that each year I was subject to termination, and it seemed that one had to demonstrate subservience in order to be retained. Perhaps I didn't take the requirement of subservience seriously enough.

Just before one time of renewal (or not), I had organised for the rejuvenation of a staff orientation program. I had rewritten or re-arranged most of the elements, and I organised for the Vice Chancellor to film a five-minute welcome to new staff. None of this was news; everyone knew that it had to happen, and there was nothing controversial about it. However, there was one thing I didn't do. I should have gone to my manager to ask her to organise this filming.

She knew that it had to happen, and she hadn't said anything about it, and I didn't see it as important enough to involve her in it. Her involvement was unnecessary. But when she found out about it, she was furious. I still couldn't see a problem, and I told her I was just doing my job. Then, I could see that I had just thrown petrol on the fire. From an ego perspective, I had just made her irrelevant.

She sulked for weeks. Then my contract came up for renewal. It was offered to me, but this time, instead of being twelve months or two years, as they had been previously, it was five months, and it was timed to end two weeks before Christmas. I pointed out to her that this was an inconvenient time for a contract to end. She claimed that this was because of the budget necessities of the university.

I stalled. I did not sign the contract immediately. And then I noticed a new clause in the contract. There was a clause about social media, and how staff were forbidden to make negative comments about their employer on social media. I had written about this subject in my HR reports for the publishing company. It had been an occurrence in the wider business community, and businesses were perturbed about it. The new clause was seen as necessary.

I thought that such a clause was inevitable in employee contracts. However, in my own work history, I had encountered the opposite: I had been defamed by an employer on the front page of the local newspaper. I felt that an employee had a right to a similar provision: the employer undertakes that it will not malign a current or former employee in a public forum unless it is a matter of criminal activity.

Given that a contract is an agreement between two parties, the employer and the employee, I felt that I was entitled to request my current employer to insert this new clause into my contract.

Accordingly, I submitted my request to the HR department. The result was paralysis. The HR department did not know what to do.

My manager asked me on numerous occasions what was happening to my contract. I replied that the HR department had not yet addressed my query relating to the contract. The time was shortening. It was two weeks before I was to be terminated. I was looking at the university's internal notice board and noticed a job advertisement from another section of the university, a college that operated largely independently.

It was very similar to my current role, only the focus was not on staff training courses but the writing of online courses for student programs. The one they were looking at immediately was engineering. I rang up and it seemed very suitable, and I applied. In this process, I had to do something I had not done before. I told them that my current employer would not be supportive of my job application, and could they please keep it confidential? I could give them references from previous employers.

They agreed, which was not a foregone conclusion. Not only that, they actually did keep it confidential; they didn't just tell me they would in order to placate me.

The process when smoothly and I obtained an interview for the job. I felt that my credentials for the job were mostly impressive, but with one exception. The immediate concern was an engineering course. What did I have that would demonstrate that I had the aptitude for the work?

I had one thing: a transcript of my engineering studies at a university, from when I was eighteen and nineteen. That was well over thirty years ago. I photocopied it ten times, enough for every person who was likely to be on the interview panel. I answered all the questions they asked me, and none of the questions was a surprise, so I weathered it well. Then, right near the end, one of the interviewers addressed me and asked the inevitable question: This is an engineering degree. We are satisfied you can design an online course, but can you deal with engineering content? It is quite specialised.

In answer, I took out the photocopies and passed them around. I said, you can see that I have completed two years of university study for engineering, and I passed every unit, many with High Distinction. I am not claiming that my knowledge of engineering is current, but I believe I can cope with the nature and the level of the material.

I was satisfied with my career planning at this point. I had done something consciously thirty years previously, something that I thought was important, and now it would pay off. They were indeed satisfied that I could do the job, and it was given to me.

It was a “green fields” job. I had to create the online course from scratch. I was ready for this. I think that in my current role I was probably getting close to the repetitive stage: the same sorts of things, over and over again.

With less than a week to go, I could now go back to my employer and tell them that I would not be taking up the five-month contract. My manager was surprised and disappointed, but I had been put in a difficult position, and I was rightfully protecting my prospects.

Chapter 7: Veering into training and instructional design

For other reasons, I could question the adequacy of my career planning. The better paid positions in the workforce tend to be management roles, not technical roles. That is, unless one is an external agent, a consultant. For most of my working life, I did not see myself as a consultant.

As one gets older, opportunities for management roles occur. However, I had experienced rejection in applying for management roles. At the publishing company, the thinking seemed to be that the writing roles were important, and the management roles were menial, at least at the first-line level. This was reflected in the pay offered for leading technical roles. It was almost on a par with the manager roles.

That may have been so, but a first-line manager role was also a stepping stone to higher levels, so it was still important. I felt, at least at the publishing company, that I was seen as a technical expert, not as a manager or consultant. And in any case, this was gratifying. The money was not such a great motivator. We need to find our own place of balance, sufficient to preserve our sense of integrity.

It is not as if these questions are settled once and for all at any particular point. An opportunity may always come up that we don't wish to resist. It could be a role where we get the chance to retain enough hands-on work to satisfy us, as well as carrying out the management tasks. At the same time, we need to be wary of being one of those managers who can't get out of their workers' way. They are constantly interfering, not allowing their workers to enjoy the satisfaction of their work or to develop their skills. (In employment law there is an expression, that an employee is "entitled to the quiet enjoyment of their job". I think this is exquisite.)

Most of the things we have to learn in our career development are subtleties like that, not big-block goals like enrolling in a higher degree, or switching to a different company or industry.

I settled into the job at the college, and learned how to build websites for learning. They didn't have to be super-flash, but they did have to be professional, and the structure of the content had to be solid too. We worked with a teacher for each subject. They wrote the content.

I was to assess that from a design point-of-view and then implement it as an online course.

“Professional” meant that it had to look credible as a university course. The students who completed this course would receive an Associate Degree of Engineering and go part-way into a Bachelor of Engineering degree. It couldn’t come across as something childish. The tone was important. Accuracy was also very important. This became an issue, because the college didn’t yet have a grasp on what it took to produce a solid, error-free course. The work had to be of a high-enough standard to begin with, and the writing and proof-reading had to be slow enough to catch all errors. The process had to be competent, but nor could it be rushed.

As we went further along the road, with more units completed and underway with students, the managers’ patience with the production process thinned. In many human projects, there is more readiness to throw effort into mending disasters than there is to do the project properly in the first place.

Managers are often the ones at fault, the ones who think that to predict two million dollars’ profit is twice as good as predicting one million dollars’ profit. Yet, they will not have thought for one second about what difference it would take in effort or strategy to produce twice the amount of profit. But for twelve months, a team is condemned to hell to try to do so.

In thinking about career development, one may eventually collide with the real state of the workplace, such as just indicated. Mostly, people work in order to earn money, so their choices are constrained. Accordingly, they go along with policies and strategies they know are not appropriate or will not be successful. And the difficulty with this perfectly sensible course of action is that they become complicit in these defective strategies and policies.

Mostly, the problem is further up the tree. The manager proposes a generous goal because this is what is demanded by their manager.

The only salvation is that circumstances change and people come and go, so the goalposts are forever shifting. In some bumbling way, we manage to get from year to year.

If this is the ordinary context for workers, is the advice to do the minimum possible the best advice that can be given? Is career development one more stumbling farce? Should one find a position that is "good enough" and leave it at that?

This would be another reason not to have a career goal. But our difficulties are generally at the personal level rather than at the professional level. It is hard to work in a way that is worse than what you can do, because you know you are capable of better. You have to live with yourself, and there is shame in that.

It is for this reason that many people choose to "go external". They decide to be a consultant or trainer, doing some form of work that is, they like to say, "independent". In a modest way, that is what I did, when I began to work as an external writer for the publishing company. And indeed, that was liberating, because I managed my own time, and I was not involved in office discussions of matters over which I never had any control anyway.

This path is preferable for people who would rather do the work than manage other people in the doing of it. If you enjoy a task, you will lose that enjoyment once you become a manager. You have to ask yourself, then, how you are going to compensate yourself for the loss. As I have noted, some managers do not resolve the problem, they simply interfere in their employees' work. Often, they make it even worse by criticising their employees' standard of work, or the way they do it. Their criticisms may or may not be valid. Often, they are not.

Some managers work it out by keeping a slice of work for themselves. In some schools, you see that the principal or the deputy principal retains a class of students, despite their busy schedule. They are not doing it because they like having too much work, they are doing it because they like the nature of the work, and it makes up for the gruelling nature of some of their administrative tasks.

There is the thought that in a perfect world, we wouldn't have such problems. You would find the situation which had the perfect in-built balance. But the balance is seldom in the external situation, it is in the balance you arrive at in your own person. And it can take time and effort to find this balance.

So, it is not the career plan that needs attention, it is your own balance with all the factors in your situation. You can accept this if you accept that the career goal may be fluid. The situation is constantly changing, and your needs are evolving over time, so the place you need to get to will likewise change. Why else would a person get restless after being in the same job for several years?

They have long experience of doing the job, the challenge of it lessens, and the mind looks around to see what else might be possible. Having a job is not a static thing; it is living. It is not about filling a box in a grid, it is about maintaining a living function. It is not static; it is about how to remain in movement. Life is always about growth and movement. The only reason it isn't is when people are suppressed. They are frozen because they see no alternatives to continuing the same job for the same employer year after year.

For those who remain contentedly in the same role, the challenge is probably in the relationships it offers.

For a teacher, the challenge may be in the new cohorts of children who come along, and the changes he/she can see in them. The curriculum may be adjusted because of changing factors in the education system, technology and social factors. So it is different each year; it is not simply repetition.

I saw the same with my mother, who was a dressmaker. The people who came along and wanted dressmaking or tailoring were different. Their needs were different, and fashion continually evolved, and it kept her engaged. Some types of work faded out, and others replaced them. It was ever a moving feast.

Then there was the year she wanted to do something different, so she went to college and learned how to do cake-decorating. She began to decorate cakes for people in the neighbourhood: twenty-first birthday cakes, wedding cakes, anniversaries. She found it interesting and she connected to the local community in a new way.

It is easy to see that there was an inner drive at work here. How she understood that and expressed it over the years evolved. She could see the connections between dressmaking and cake-decorating too. She was doing something artistic, and it served people on big occasions in their lives.

How it fitted into her life also changed. She had paid off the mortgage on her house, and the economic threat of being in debt was lifted. She enjoyed what she did in a new way.

The joys of a fulfilled career are of the same type, even where the scale, the complexity and the risks are much greater.

But how could you change things? How could you extend yourself to meet a new challenge? It is important to stay alive. I have known people who earned their living as a craftsperson, and they always managed to extend their skills each year. I knew a cabinetmaker who made high-quality period-reproduction furniture, who worked on commission, but somehow he managed to take on projects that required skills he didn't have, and he learned. His carving became more exquisite, he explored different countries and periods (such as French seventeenth century), and he made different types of furniture (such as a grandfather clock). Always, there was something he had not done before.

For myself, now at the college, new challenges came along. After the engineering course, I was asked to create online courses in the Arts field. This required different strengths. The engineering had required attention to exercises to build skills in mathematics and physics. The Arts units required a discursive structure of content that connected to other readings, and left scope for online discussions.

At the same time, COVID occurred, and suddenly all the teachers needed to know how to conduct online discussion forums. This became a central focus for our group. We devised a training program for teachers, so that they would be familiar with the steps and be able to carry them out confidently.

This likewise became an opportunity to establish sound teaching principles. Most of the teachers had no background in teaching. They had a Masters degree or a PhD in a particular subject area, and it was simply assumed that they could teach. The observation of our team (we had all had experience as teachers) was that they could all talk, but they couldn't teach effectively. Nor could they check for understanding. And they couldn't design content for learning. These are not skills that we all intuitively have.

It was a very satisfying period of time. We had an opportunity that does not normally exist, courtesy of the pandemic. We were not overbearing about our offering; it simply fitted into a course that was suddenly necessary. We were able to take small groups of teachers through online discussion forums, giving them the opportunity to lead discussions themselves before they had to lead groups of students, and we saw their growth in confidence.

We supplemented that hands-on experience with a set of basic principles of teaching and learning. I think that most of the teachers were grateful for the chance to undergo the course. It would not normally have happened at all. The college itself accepted this offering with gratitude. It stood up to scrutiny and it enhanced the college's reputation.

In all this work, there was still the question of whether the work was in harmony with my "inner drive". Yes, teaching had always been a theme of my work life, but was I happy with where I had ended up? One writer put the question this way: "When you return to the source, will you be satisfied that you've completed your life on earth?"

You can substitute your own expression for "return to the source". To put it in a modern frame, at the end of your working life, will you be satisfied that you have fulfilled your career goals?

My goal had always been about writing rather than teaching, from when I was a young age, still at primary school. So, yes, at the college, I was doing some writing, especially the course for teachers on teaching. It made use of wide areas of my learning, that I had acquired over many years; it wasn't simply a product of my job description.

But could it answer my question? Was it ultimately satisfying, as the outcome of my entire working life? Some people have the concept that your working life should have something you can call a "great work". Did I have a great work?

Note, this does not have to be something that still exists. My mother made clothes and decorated cakes. The clothes wore out, the cakes were cut up and consumed. That was in the nature of those things. But my mother held a worthy role in her community through those activities. For that, she could be satisfied.

For me, there were some things that I was happy to call a great work. The training and development manual that I kept going for about fifteen years was a worthy piece of work. Over that period of time, I wrote or rewrote the entire 1,600 pages, covering the whole scope of training in organisations, as well as the management of the training department. I wrote entire new sections that addressed emerging aspects of training, such as online learning.

It was a worthy service to training professionals. I continually grew my knowledge and kept it up to date. I attended industry events and I listened. In the context I was in, it was the utmost I could do. I could be satisfied with what I had done.

And yet, I always knew that I was writing in a given context for a given purpose, and it wasn't everything that was in my mind. If I wasn't inside that context, what would I do then? I had been aware for a long time that saying you are a writer is one statement, but it leaves hanging the next question: what do you write? Or, what do you write about?

PART 2: BEING A WRITER (OR NOT)

Chapter 8: The child chooses to be a writer

There was a parallel writer's life that ran alongside the career I have described above. I want to describe that now. It was, for the most part, in the background, and it was sometimes in tension with the life I was living. It began with elements I mentioned above, that expressed my frustration as a young person with not being able to find a paid living, or a livelihood, as a writer.

I note that I had already placed restrictions on myself, and perhaps if I had had a suitable vocational guidance counsellor or mentor, my life would have been different. But I disallow this statement. The fact is, we are all subject to our inner drive, and mine told me, clearly and adamantly, that I did not want to be a journalist. I recognise now that it would have been very sensible to be a journalist for a while, because I would have been schooled in writing.

As it was, I was in in my late forties before I got to the publishing company and was subject to a regular regimen of writing, the period I call my apprenticeship. This was true even though I was a mature person, I had almost a decade's experience as a manager, and I had a degree with first class honours in business, and the degree was heavily weighted towards law.

Have I been true to my inner drive, all in all? For my life now, I would say that I am, and I can describe my journey towards this place. But it is arguable that it was not so in my early adulthood. However, it is subject to argument, and I will argue the point. It hinges on whether it is possible to have a career plan, and what difference that could make. Or does it depend on how we define a career plan?

It could be considered a great irony that when I was working for the university, I wrote two online programs for career development: one for academics, and one for professional staff. I had a reference committee with whom I consulted, but they gave me free scope, and I made use of material that I had written in earlier times. One of my best sources was the manual on training and development that I wrote for so many years for the publishing company.

I have mentioned some aspects of writing in my childhood and adolescence. I would say my attraction to writing began in infants' class. One day I brought home a drawing I had made, and showed it to my mother. My mother laughed. She said that all of my heads were square.

I was a bit disappointed. I liked my drawing. I suppose I mulled over this disappointment. Another day, I had another disappointment. We had been given a large blank sheet of paper and a pencil, and the teacher toldus, "Take your pencil for a walk". Then passed several minutes, during which time my alarm rose. I wanted to draw something, not wander aimlessly over a large sheet of paper.

But, how does one draw something if one can't lift up the pencil? We were not to lift up the pencil. Consequently, when we were told to hold up our sheet of paper, I had a crowded mass of line stuck up in the top left-hand corner of the sheet. My teacher was disappointed. She said, "You could have used all of the sheet. You didn't have to stay stuck up in one corner like that."

She pointed to some of the other children's work. They had run all over the sheet. I, on the other hand, thought, "Why?" and now I thought, "You didn't tell us that before."

Combined, these two episodes made me think I was not good at art, and I should forget about it. What could I be, then? It took me some time, but I was progressing well in infants' class apart from my unsatisfactory art. I enjoyed reading and writing. When I was in first class, the teachers decided early in the year that I might as well go up to second class, and I did. I was still ahead of most children in the class in reading and writing.

From then on, I did well at school, and my reading and writing were advanced. It was in primary school that I took a memorable step towards writing. We had a library class, and we had a book for library lessons, and I started making up poems and copying them down in the back of the book. There was one day when the library teacher discovered this, and I spent an anxious minute when I wondered if I was in trouble.

However, she was in a hurry, and decided it wasn't worth worrying about. She passed over it. That was a relief. I hadn't had the thought that the teacher might discover the poems and be displeased. So, it was like being given passive permission to continue.

As I went into high school, my personal writing was primarily poetry. It was about beauty and feelings. It was a hidden thing, hidden from my family and most other people. An exception was in the second year of high school, when we had an English class where we were asked to write a poem. I had a few rhyming poems about nature in my exercise books (I now had more than one book, and they were dedicated solely to the purpose of poetry). I had written these poems as exercises, because one has to learn.

When other children in the class realised that I had poems, some of them wanted one that they could hand in as their own. I said no, but there was a girl at the time to whom I gave one. Thus, it became known that I wrote poems. I explored different types of poems: ballads, sonnets, lyrical verse, free verse, modernist verse. I explored emotions: wonder, angst, cynicism.

All of this activity was helpful to me. It was a form of expression that would not have occurred otherwise. Did anyone see them? Over the high school years, there were a few friends whom I allowed to read them. Sometimes I would make copies, writing them out by hand, and give them away to friends or people I knew (and trusted). But it was separate from the boy who was growing up and who had to make a choice of career.

There were only two occupations where writing was central: journalist and academic. I had already made up my mind about being a journalist. I did not want to be a person who wrote about news affairs and politics. I knew there were other things that journalists wrote about, but nor did I want to be a person who wrote about things I considered trivial. You could accuse me of being high-minded.

As to being an academic, that seemed a bit far removed from my life. I didn't know anyone like that. What kind of academic would I be? I didn't know. History? English? I didn't think I could aim to be anything higher than a teacher. And I didn't know about other fields. I thought that to be at university, one had to be a practitioner of some kind first. For example, one might be a lawyer first and then go to university to teach law. At this stage, I did not know about psychology, sociology, philosophy or other subjects.

Nor did I want to completely cut myself off from the society in which I had grown up. I did not want to join an aloof class. I did not think that would be "better", whatever that might mean.

Yet, at high school, I proved myself to be a good writer. For English, I wrote sound essays about the books we read. I wrote some long essays; I could do the research, explore different perspectives, and carry a train of thought to an interesting conclusion. At the end of high school, I was first in English. But still, I knew of no occupations where this would be a central skill, especially when thinking of a young person.

There was another form of writing that I practised in my teen years. It was quite a particular form of writing. I was in the Boy Scouts, and I was a keen participant; I took it seriously. The Boy Scouts rewarded such an attitude by having a wide range of badges that one could earn. There were badges for bushwalking and camping as well as various crafts and hobbies. I achieved most of the badges that it was possible to obtain.

In my writing box, I have the logbooks for seven hikes and one for the Camp Warden's Badge. The other badges were for First Class Journey (the junior step into the Scouts from the Cubs), Bushwalker's and Pathfinder's. There were logs for hikes that were not for badges. Some of these were for more adventurous trips, such as a one-day trip that involved abseiling down a canyon into a creek bed and walking out the lower end. This involved floating down one section on air mattresses.

Another trip was a five-day walk down in the Snowy Mountains starting at Guthega. This happened because, as I got older, some of the youths who were older than me had car licences, and the more fortunate ones had cars. We also went on a trip to some caves and a ghost town, Yerranderie.

The logs I wrote were meticulous, and nicely set out, all handwritten, of course, and including hand-drawn topographical maps I copied out from the real maps. The later logbooks included black-and-white photos. I also drew sketches that would be called crude, but the maps were beautiful. The logbooks contained dates, places, distance of the hike, companions on the hike, the map used (named properly). They included menus for food, ration lists, equipment taken.

The logbook for the Bushwalker's badge was forty pages long. The bulk of it was set out with three columns at the left, for time, distance from the last point, and compass direction. The fourth column was the descriptive notes: what the track was like, the vegetation, the weather, the steepness, distinctive features and anything else of interest. They describe where we camped, and any decisions we had to make when we were unsure.

I also recorded the birds we saw, and the trees: I could recognise most of them, although not with full botanical names. At the end of the log, I would compile a list of all the birds we saw, and any other animals. On one hike, we saw half a dozen lyre birds.

I was consciously developing my competency. I don't know how the standard of my logbooks compared to those of other boys. It didn't really matter; I wasn't aiming to be better than other boys. I wanted my work to be excellent, or as close to perfection as possible. My standard was the ideals of Baden-Powell, the man who started the Boy Scouts in 1907.

I suppose most boys would have thrown their logbooks out once they had finished with the Boy Scouts. Why would you keep them? But for me, the logbooks were an aspect of my life as a writer.

My logbooks are also of interest for what they reveal about the death of my father. My father died in early March 1967. January 1967 was when I went on the big adventure to the Snowy Mountains, and in February I went on the abseiling trip up to the Blue Mountains. There was nothing more until August 1967, which was when I went to Yerranderie. This was the last trip. Some things come to a close.

There was one other thing. It is to do with the badges. Among the array of badges that we could attempt to do, there was one related to art. I was not going to do that. But, I went to the scoutmaster and said, "No, I can't do that, but I can write poetry. If I can demonstrate that, can you devise a way for me to obtain a badge for it?"

He wasn't against the idea, but he said, "I can't do that, but I will talk to the Akela (leader) that you had in the cubs. I know she writes stories for the magazine that is distributed to schools. She will think of something." (She also had a brother who was a professor at a university.)

So, the Akela worked out what I should do, to parallel the requirements of the artistic version of the badge. I had to show that I had read a variety of poets, and different kinds of poetry. I had to show that I knew something about the life of three poets, I had to read a poem, and I had to show some poems I had written. I also had to show that this activity had been going on for some time; I had not just dreamed it up in the past week.

I don't remember the details of what I showed her, but I do remember that I was able to satisfy her that I was serious about what I was doing, and I was not without merit. This was another step in my affirmation of myself as a writer.

And my father died, the great disruption was happening with The Beatles and rock music, the American revolution in music was happening, the monstrous spectacle of Vietnam was happening, Australia joined in, conscription started, and that threat loomed over me. The threat of nuclear war also loomed. And in 1972, *Time* magazine published the first report on climate change, a report which argued that it might make the planet unliveable. I cut the article out of the magazine and kept it.

Despair was all around, and yet the music of The Beatles was suggesting (loudly) that life might be worth living. My decision to study engineering after high school was an attempt to hold onto something stable. A career plan has to acknowledge the dramas of life.

So, there was the life that was necessary to live, studying engineering, and there was my life on the side, which included writing poetry, wrestling with the religion in which I had grown up, riding a motorcycle, and playing the guitar and writing songs. I was never in a band; I just played guitar at home. There were a couple of occasions when I sang songs of mine in public.

I thought some of my songs were not bad. But it was yet another life on the side, filled with longing and frustration, but also with enjoyment. Part of the internal wrestle was about being up in the public eye. I was not confident, but nor did I think I had a great voice, so I was happy to be in the background. There were a couple of songs where there was a brief possibility that someone else would perform them, but this did not happen.

On another front, there was a magazine that was distributed among churches across Sydney, and I was asked to be on the committee and to write articles for it. That was a good experience, which lasted for a couple of years. The magazine was generally conservative, although the articles tended to be thoughtful. It was my first experience of writing within a context and producing material that was suitable for it.

Amidst the ferment of the time, some more broadly spiritual magazines and newspapers started up. There was one that had a column for music. I had just heard an album by the progressive rock group, Yes (the album was "Tales from Topographic Oceans") and I asked the editor if he would be interested in a review of that album. He said yes, and I wrote the article, and he published it.

It was a difficult album to write about, because it was difficult to understand. It was about worlds and trials and possibility, spread across two records. It was vast, symphonic, about wonder and glory, exalted above the mess that we were living in. Perhaps the editor published it because he could see that I loved it. This was an isolated event; I did not become a regular writer about music albums.

There was, however, a larger gig. I was attending what was called an alternative Christian group. It was for people who still aligned with Christianity, but who felt rebellious about the church, and also wanted to respond to the social ferment in the world. It attracted a large following, and it started its own newspaper, distributing thousands of copies around Australia.

I asked to go on the committee which organised each issue. I wanted to write, and this avenue would voice my concerns. What was happening in society? What direction should we be heading in? I was accepted onto the committee, and I wrote a lot for the paper over a couple of years. My articles were given a good airing.

The group also began to run training courses for young leaders. I was well-read, and I contributed to the writing of these courses, and in their delivery. This was all gratifying, and I added a perspective that other people didn't have. But here I was in a large group of people, and there were points of view there that I did not wish to be aligned with. Was I to argue with them? Was I to claim that I knew best?

No, not those things. But in getting involved with this group, I had severed my ties with my former church, and I had moved too far. I couldn't go back. And during this period, there was the motorbike accident.

In all those months in hospital, I did not write much. I had a notebook, but I didn't feel like writing a diary of the experience. I didn't feel that I had gained much in wisdom. I didn't feel like producing a story of salvation, although there was a story of salvation within this experience. At one point, four weeks after the accident, my leg had gangrene and the doctors thought the leg might have to be amputated.

When they went to operate, the gangrene was gone. They couldn't explain it. But I had had a huge shift in my outlook in the previous week. A minister who held healing services had come to see me, and told me to stop being a martyr. The universe did not want me to be one-legged. He told me to put my energy into being whole. That was how to live.

It woke me up. He was right; that was how I had been looking at the situation. And there it was: it was the end of the week and the gangrene was gone.

I still spent months in the hospital, because extensive skin grafts were required on my leg. But, I had two legs, not one. I would be whole again.

The other thought in my mind was that in the Christian group, I would be harnessed. I would be featured in the newspaper as a miracle which proved everything the newspaper wanted to say. I would have a voice, but it would no longer be mine. And although I had read a lot, I still didn't understand what was going on in society. I knew it would be best for me to be silent.

So, I underwent the skin grafts, I wrote poems occasionally (but I did not keep a regular diary), and when I was out of hospital and I could walk again, I went on a journey in Tasmania by myself.

However, I have revisited the book that contained the diary I kept in hospital, and the poems, such as they were. Although what I have written above is true, it glosses over the story of that time. I struggled, and I found it hard to articulate what was happening, or who I was now. On one day, early on, I wrote: "I am criminal: I have my pen in my hand but there are no words in my head." A cold passage I had of it.

When I actually counted the poems, there were close to forty of them for the year. However, most of them are awkward and cheerless. In recent years, I went through my early poetry, the period from childhood to my thirties, and selected some for a book. It was called *That Was Then: The Early Poems Project*. I had a section for the year of the motorbike accident, so there were some poems from hospital.

The exercise book with the diary and the poems has a tabulation on the inside cover. I had counted off the days all the time I was in hospital, in groups of seven (for weeks), not five. On the many days when I could manage nothing else, I did check off the day. I did write, at one point, that my lack of diarising was laziness, but I also noted that it was lack of concentration.

I noted that most of the nurses were kind. They were busy and efficient, but they were also sympathetic. One nurse copied me out two poems, which are inside the diary book. They are wonderful pieces. The first is by e.e. cummings: "one winter afternoon". The other piece was written by Zbigniew Herbert, a Polish post-War poet and essayist. It is called "Elephant".

They were both extraordinary pieces and they touched me deeply. I muddled on, taking what comfort I could from the nurses and from intermittent visitors. There was a great deal at stake; if the skin graft did not work, my leg was still in question. But the doctors believed that things would go well. I wrote, "Heaven must be here someplace."

Late in the year, I was out of hospital, I had been back at work (teaching), and I was trying to figure out what was the same and what had changed. My sister was living in Tasmania, and she announced that she was getting married, so I went to Hobart in December. After the wedding, I hitch-hiked around the island by myself, and I met people from around the world.

I enjoyed the mountains and the ocean, I enjoyed the wilderness. I didn't have much to say about it, although strangely, after having been in hospital for months and never writing much at all, on this trip I kept a diary. I wrote some poems too. Mostly, I had moments of living.

One day, I was picked up by a couple in a panel van and we were driving along the road when they stopped. Why? We had been following a truck full of a fresh crop of peas, and a clump of peas had fallen off. They stopped and we all got out. They said, "You have to try these. You will never taste fresher peas than this." I had never tasted raw peas before. We had always cooked them, and I thought this was how things were done.

This simple experience brought me to tears. The entire trip was similarly moving. When I came home, I put the diary away. I had a box with my writing in it. I always kept that box. It had my primary school library book in it, and everything since. I didn't look at the diary again for over forty years.

Chapter 9: The adult earns a livelihood

Also, after I came home, I got together with the lady who soon became my wife. I had been dribbling along with the Bachelor of Arts degree, although I had had the year off because of the accident. My lady was working, so for a while I went to university full-time. However, it coincided with the time when the university had descended into chaos.

In one burst of energy, I wrote a long article about the concept of authority for the student newspaper. It was called "Authority and Experience". One might think this was a bit abstract, but it was the central issue of the day, so it was very relevant. They published it across a centre-page spread.

It didn't lead to anything else, although I think the reaction to it was generally thoughtful. In those days I was anxious for one thing to lead to other things. Nowadays I treat such endeavours as an event rather than the beginning of a process.

Looking back at the article, it had the brashness of youth and was occasionally pompous, but the thread of argument was basically sound, and I would say it is largely consistent with my current thinking. I am grateful for the time I spent in these years trying to sort out what I thought, and how I wanted to live.

However, I was becoming concerned about the chaos in which I was trying to study. I wasn't optimistic that the chaos would lead to anything better. When my girlfriend told me she was pregnant, I took it as a good excuse to discontinue. I accepted that I had to work for a living. It was an accepted fact of life. I had been teaching for three years. I would return to work.

When I discontinued my studies, I took up psychiatric nursing. It was a temporary mission, essentially, to find about hidden aspects of life. But I was also mulling over the idea of leaving the city. I was thinking to go a long way away from Sydney, and my girlfriend had relatives in regional Queensland, so I applied for a job teaching there. I was successful, and at the end of the year we packed up our modest pile of belongings and left.

We settled in the coastal city, far north of Brisbane, and I again settled into teaching, although I still did not feel that it was my life's purpose. But I did not find much time or motivation for writing. I did not know what audience I would be writing to, so I did not know what I might write. I was as clear as ever that there were many strands of writing that were not for me. I was not a novelist, even though I enjoyed reading novels regularly.

I was still an occasional poet. When we stopped moving around and found a place to settle, I wrote about my feelings about this life: "Song for adopted land", "The winding way", "Yarns of the new settlers" were some of them. After I started writing novels, many years later, after 2009, I wrote a novel which was about my journey to the bush and back to the city, and I included some of these poems.

For the time being, I typed out my poems (I now had a typewriter) and put them in a folder in the box. In that sense I was being true to myself. I did not share them with others, except occasionally I might send a couple of poems to a friend to read. Mostly, these friends were at a distance, and I mailed them. Occasionally they might tell me that they liked what I had sent. But this was all like small noise in the background.

I accepted that these were busy years. When you have children, you need to attend to them and give time to them. The young years are intense learning years, and they are years that children should enjoy.

I ended my years as an unemployed, country-dwelling hippie. I got the job at the Catholic high school and gradually "came back in" to society. I had not changed my ideas about the difficulties of modern city life, and the bleakness of relentless industrialisation and rampant capitalism, but I had no illusions that I and my fellow bush-dwellers could create anything much better. It would be positive merely because it was low consumption. I settled down to doing the best I could in my chosen community, at a closer level. I did not think I could change the world, except in a small way, by living well.

There was the event of my wife leaving, with the children, and moving far away, twelve hours by car. I was not going to follow; that seemed senseless. I stayed in my house. I continued to work, teaching at the school. I sat and thought a lot, and avoided drinking too much.

While I was teaching at the school, I was involved in producing a book, which I suppose I can regard as my first book. Another teacher and I taught the manual arts courses, and the principal asked us to prepare the book as the written program of all these courses. We had lesson plans and we had discussed the content of these, but they had not, to date, been compiled. This was needed for the purposes of the education department.

The program covered woodwork, wood machining, metalwork and metal machining, plastics, ceramics, and leatherwork. The program book was 120 pages long, and bound in book form, with several copies made. So, even here in a non-career job, I was meeting my inner drive.

At home, I began writing short stories: stories about people I invented, people who belonged in the valley in a fantasised way. Some of the stories were almost fables, and I liked them. These too, I typed up and put in the box. I did not expect an audience for them. Was I writing magical realism? I didn't have that terminology then, and the term may not add much to our understanding. In the last decade, in my writing years, I showed one of these stories to a friend, and the reaction was, "I loved it. I want to read more."

But there was no more, at least not to that story. I had not extended the story further, despite my love for it. The most I have done is to include a few of the stories at the end of one of my books, the one called *To the Bush and Back to Business*. This is the one that also has some poems in it.

There was also one children's story, a story that I wrote after the birth of my last child. It was a whimsical story that featured books, called "Senior Owl and the Biscuit Factory". It also went back into the box. I did not see myself as an illustrator.

However, I did encounter a lady who was an illustrator. She lived with her boyfriend a couple of valleys over from me. I took some poems to her, she showed me some of her work, and we talked. We were fishing for a connection to each other. She was Swiss, and for me, her drawings evoked the idea of Swiss fairy tales. They were lovely, and done lovingly but, apart from Senior Owl, I was not writing children's stories.

There was also the fact that her boyfriend was very jealous and overbearing. I could not see she and I working well together. We did not pursue the liaison.

The main work of this decade was the writing of stories. I had seldom written stories when I was younger, so it was a question of exploring new directions. What lay at the end of it? I did not know, but between relationships, I had the time to explore.

One of my initiatives was to undertake a correspondence course in short story writing. It was a constructive experience. I received lecture notes, which enabled me to think about what I was doing and what I wanted to do, and I had to write short stories to submit. I received feedback on the stories.

I found it difficult to be objective about what I was doing. This may have been because I had not made a commitment to write a certain type of stories. I wasn't interested in writing romance or westerns, detective stories or thrillers. I didn't feel that I could write science fiction or fantasy. But I wrote stories, over thirty of them. It was enjoyable to sit on the lounge-room floor at night, especially in winter when the fire was going, and see where the characters took me.

Eventually, I had to get a bigger box to put all the writing in.

While I was in my quiet period, contemplating my failed marriage, society, the future and all of life, I got all my poems out of the box: exercise books, folders and stray notes, and decided to compile a collection. I had no way of publishing it, but I had the idea, and ideas can gather momentum. This went on for some weeks, and at the end of it, I had decided on two collections. They were themed a bit differently, but they were from more-or-less the same period of time, namely, about 1967 to 1980.

Then, the two collections went back into the box, and stayed there for several years more. I was still pondering my career plans, as opportunities came along. Successively, I changed from being a teacher to being a project officer for unemployed youth, a community profile officer for the nearby local council, a coordinator of adult education, and the general manager of a community organisation that provided a variety of services for people with disabilities.

The role of community profile officer had required research and writing skills. During the twelve months or so, I produced an extensive report on the community from the perspective of human needs. I ensured that my data was sound, my logic was solid, and my conclusions and recommendations were succinct and feasible. I did more than was asked of me, because I had the capacity, and I thought I should make the most of the opportunity.

I produced a community services directory, a report on housing, and a proposal for a service for unemployed youth (the same as the one in which I had been employed). My recommendations were mostly taken up, and resulted in successful new community endeavours. I knew that for ideas to result in success, there has to be enthusiasm and collaboration between people, but I also felt that clear writing was invaluable in laying the foundation for achievable projects.

The manager job came along soon after this job ended. It was a leap forward in complexity and stature, responsibility and risk. But correspondingly, I was lean on imagination for poetry. The writing I did as a manager was functional, and dependent on an informed knowledge base. Yes, my reports had to be lucid, but I also had to be schooled in the structure and phrasing of the reports and submissions. I learned. I refined my skills.

I was also fully engaged in my work. I felt that I was producing something positive in the community, and I was willing to submit myself to this work.

However, after two years, a writing project arose that I couldn't resist. The local council (not in the same town as my work) wanted to produce a history of the shire, and they advertised for someone. It was another unlikely advertisement that I thought was pointed directly towards me.

The advertisement was in the form of a request for tender. I had never responded to any kind of tender before, and if I hadn't been keen, I would not have bothered. I had to make up what I was prepared to accept to take on this project. Essentially, what it amounted to was the price of a decent computer (for 1988), a printer, and a small allowance for travel around the shire.

I finished the book in time for it to be printed and launched at a festival near the end of the year. I worked hard this year, harder than usual, because this project was happening in tandem with my full-time job. It was ridiculous to think that I could do it, but I managed. I worked nights and weekends.

I had a rough idea about the history of the shire, but it is another thing to be precise, coherent and fluent. There was only one previous book on the history of the shire, and it had been what is called a "coffee table" book, which had been done about thirty years earlier. There were a couple of regional histories, and the aboriginal history had been barely mentioned.

I wanted to do justice to the shire, as I lived there now and I loved the place. I could also see that people here loved the place too. And it was a big shire, so I had to consider all its far reaches as well. I was well aware that I was not a historian, but nor was I being asked to undertake a critical analysis of the history of the shire for an academic treatise.

I was being asked to tell the story in a way that was inclusive and accessible. I felt that it was too easy for local histories to confine themselves to the story of the dominant classes: the squatters, the big farmers, the political leaders, the main-street merchants. I lived in the house of a man who had been a small, steady dairy farmer for a generation, and I lived at a time when the natural beauty of the hills and valleys was being rediscovered.

Without being sentimental, I wanted to convey my respect for everyone's part in the story, and how the shire established its own identity in the modern world with a minimum of egotistical bombast. There were dairy farmers, timbermen, bridge-builders, carriers, the man who started the hardware store, the man who started the newspaper, there were farm-wives, nurses, and families who lived with a great deal of independence.

The book traversed the development of the towns, the milestones, and disasters such as fires and floods. I provided the facts, but more importantly, I told the story. It was well-received, and it sold very well. I was pleased: pleased that I had finished it in the time frame, pleased with the story, and the accuracy of it, and pleased with the final product, which featured many great photographs.

I did not see the project as leading to anything else. It was a unique project. I had simply been the right person in the right place at the right time. It had been a good exercise in logistics as well, organising my time and effort, organising my materials, and organising my relations with other people.

In the period after the book had been completed, I began to see that my computer held many other possibilities too. I had a box full of poems and stories, I even had two collections of poems. Although most of it was typed, it wasn't digitised. I set to work typing everything again. It was magic to be able to save files, and to complete and check one's work on-screen before one sent it to the printer.

I even invested in desktop publishing software. I did a layout for the two collections of poems. I also did a layout for the story of Senior Owl; no pictures, but a cover and a page layout for the text. For one of the poetry collections, I took the print-out to town and got a few copies made. But having done that, I was lost for what to do next. It wasn't enough to justify having a book launch. They went back into the box.

Only recently, last month, I was putting one of my books back on the bookshelf when I noticed a thin volume. It was the version of Senior

Owl that I had made all those years ago. I had forgotten all about it. Perhaps it is not too late to return to it.

I did not have much time to think about writing beyond this small indulgence. I was still engrossed in my manager's job, and time had sped up. The projects were getting bigger, we had more staff, and the complications were growing. I was coming into the time when conflict would break out, and I would be the target of lies and hostility. I rode the horse to the bitter end.

Does one become embroiled in troubles because one is in the wrong place? There is a school of thought that thinks so. Can I link all of my problems back to choosing the wrong career to start with, and not correcting my path along the way? And if I say "No", is that simply an act of self-justification?

I do not know how I would have "corrected my path". When would I have done it? There were points of inflexion in the past: when I first left the city, when I left to live in the bush, when I went back to teaching, when I left one or other of the jobs I had occupied since then. At any point I could have made a different choice. And it has to be admitted that at most of these points, I was responsible for a family. (The women were choices too. I could have made different choices there.)

It is generally not constructive to try to deconstruct the past, as if the present "you" can revisit any of those places in the past and make a different decision. We have a past. We can think more kindly of it, or we can be more critical of it, but we cannot change it otherwise. What can we do now? Moreover, what do we want to do now?

I spent time at home in the valley, licking my wounds after the sacking. I even went to the Industrial Relations Commission and argued against my sacking, and I was successful, but when I thought about it, did I really want to go back and work for the people who had sacked me? That would have been truly unwise.

Sometimes it is better to lose.

Eventually I made the decision to go back to university. Once I had the idea of getting a Bachelor of Business degree, I must say, I liked it. And the experience itself was very enjoyable. I think I am naturally a student. I had certainly enjoyed the job for the council where I had to prepare a profile of the whole community and its needs. And being a student meant writing essays on various topics. it was like the best years of school, all over again.

So, in a way, life settled down for a while, a couple of years. The seasons passed, life was enjoyable, occasionally neighbours had get-togethers. Then there was a surprise. I was contacted by the local primary school and asked if I was interested in writing a history of the school. It was to be a hundred years old the next year. They would offer me an honorarium.

What this meant was that people in the community recognised me as a writer, at least in the sense that I could research and put together a creditable history of the school, and they trusted me with such a project. I could see that the people on the committee were all excited about the event. They were all ex-pupils of the school, and they still held it in warm regard.

I agreed to the project. I could see that the core of the project would be to work with the local people, and hear what it was they loved about the school. I realised that many of them had photos they wanted to share. Some of them also had stories they had written, or they had asked an ex-teacher who now lived somewhere else to write a story about their time at the school.

It was a most enjoyable twelve months, and the book came together readily. I used an A4 format so that I could have large photos. One of the delightful episodes was the taking of a photo of all the school's pupils in the school playground. They organised the photographer, and waited for a day that was going to be sunny. They set up all the classes in just the right way.

What they were doing was replicating a photo that had been taken of the whole school in 1927. Everyone, teachers and pupils, were excited about the photo for days, and of course, the two photos featured prominently in the book.

The format I used was a magazine format, because I had a main story, and then I had numerous vignettes, such as one on how children travelled to school in the old days (which were not so long ago). The featured photo for that story was a horse with six children on it. They were all siblings, and the horse took them all to school every day, with no adult. It was a tame horse.

On the day of the fair, an ABC radio program came to the school and broadcast from the site. There were many conversations between people who had not seen each other for years. It was a community still very much alive. I was pleased to have played a part in it all.

I had one conundrum after the publication of the book: what was I to do with the pile of articles I had received from people in the surrounds or from afar? I had referred to some of them in the book, but I was unable to do more than that. But these articles had been contributed for the purpose of the school's one-hundredth anniversary, so I didn't think that I should simply ignore them.

There were twenty-six articles, varying in length from two to fifteen pages. The authors were ex-pupils and ex-teachers. I talked to the committee about it and said I was prepared to compile the articles into a bound volume if they could organise a few copies to be printed. There should be a copy for each author, and some copies for the libraries of the primary school, the high school, and maybe some of the feeder primary schools.

This was agreed to, and I prepared the volume. It was not fancy, but it was professional. I think it did justice to all the stakeholders. It contained no writing of mine, but it honoured other people who had put their hand to writing.

Chapter 10: Writing comes to the fore

Was I a writer? Yes, undoubtedly. I was a writer of history. I was a writer of student essays on business topics. I was a writer of research reports and business submissions. I could turn my hand to a community newsletter. And in a box at home, I had a pile of poems and short stories. Was it enough? And what, to me, was the most important?

"Have a goal in life. Have a purpose, and your life will be purposeful. Have a meaning and your life will be meaningful. Persevere and be flexible." That was what one writer said.

I continued with my business degree, and I completed the honours year. I was awarded a medal. I began applying for jobs outside of my home town. I felt I would have to go back to the city. And as it happened, my university record was enough for a publishing company to think I was an appropriate person to be a writer and editor for them, on management and employment law.

When I took up the work, I settled into it quickly and was accepted as a competent writer, capable of producing astute and well-informed commentary, and tuned into current needs and concerns. The opportunity came for me to undertake a Master of Education degree through work, and I had never completely let go of education in my haphazard career path, so I signed up for it.

Again, I was being a student, and I enjoyed it. I was exploring education in a way that I had not had a chance to do previously. In a way it was leapfrogging, because I was going straight to online learning instead of focusing on classroom teaching, which was now largely irrelevant to me. it was in the years that everyone was exploring online learning for the first time.

In the context I was in, it was an evolution from correspondence education, which had a respectable history of about a hundred years. This was a richer perspective than institutions that only had the experience of compliance and similar competency training. For my main project, I took the chance to write an online course on ethics for managers. It was a good opportunity.

It took several years of experience at the publishing company for me to accept that I was not producing anything that was from me personally. It was all objective and well-balanced, but it was also anonymous. It lacked the personal, experiential perspective.

I was living in the city, and it was over twenty years since I had compiled the two collections of poems. But I still had the box. It was stashed in the corner of a room. I even had the files on a disk, but I had changed computers several times, and I no longer had a computer that could read the files. I decided that it was not an infinite job, and I sat and typed them all out again.

Technology had moved on, and so had I. I could do the layout for books. I found a company that did small print runs, and prepared the two books. (It was always going to be two books. I considered whether I should combine them into one book, but it was always going to be two books! I think our obstinacy on apparently irrational issues like this is an important, and positive, determinant of our lives.)

I had joined an organisation for writers, and it periodically held book events for writers who were launching their own books. I exhibited my two books there, and held a small book launch there as well. It was in among a large throng of other writers, but the important thing was that I was displaying my books in public, and all the poems went back to when I was living in my house in the valley. It was a good thing to do.

Having satisfied that desire, I turned my attention to something more academic. I had written about business ethics in my various publications at the publishing company, but I could not explore it in the depth I wanted. I had explored ethics through an online course for managers in my Masters degree, but I felt the need for a more extensive treatment: a book.

I had questions that I had been considering for over twenty years, and I had been developing my own perspective on them. I thought that I could produce a book that spoke to the contemporary business world.

It was not my first book, but it would be my first non-fiction book that was not about a story, a history. I had read many management books, and business ethics books, so I felt that I could develop my voice and present my point of view competently. I spent a year or two shaping the book. During this time, I thought about whether I should undertake a PhD in business ethics, but I thought that what I wanted to do would be better served by a book.

I wanted to set out a perspective on business ethics in the modern world, then present my perspective on human values as an approach to ethics. Following this, I wanted to talk about how managers could implement ethics in their organisation. I thought of this latter aspect as pastoral, and I thought that that would be considered inappropriate in a PhD thesis. However, it should find a place in the book market.

Having completed the book, I found a few people to read it and recommend it. With this, I approached a number of publishing companies. None of them was interested. One of them asked me if I was a lecturer in business ethics, and how many hundred students did I have, and would I be recommending or requiring them to purchase it?

I decided to publish the book myself, committing to a small print run. I decided to start a website, and I had been approaching professional organisations to speak about my distinctive approach to business ethics. I did manage to speak at numerous events, with managers, human resource folk and trainers. I sold a few books.

I wouldn't call this initiative a great success, although I retained my faith in what the book was articulating. However, I also wanted to see if I could get published in academic journals. I had some successes here, addressing narrow questions that a paper could address adequately. I also had numerous successes with articles for business magazines.

The driver for my ethics book had been the situation I had faced as a manager in the community organisation. Over the years, numerous people had suggested to me that I should write about it, as an account of the events. The issues were universal. But I had thought that no one would be interested in the story of some bad people in a small town a long time ago. All the people were gone, the organisation had moved on, and so had I.

Further, I could not see how I could write that story. I conceived of it as a parallel to a local history book, requiring facts, dates, places, and people's names. I thought that all I would get would be lawsuits for defamation. In any case, I didn't want to be trawling over that kind of minutiae for months. The whole thing would take ages and, just, no....

However, there was a new twist. One of my sons suggested that I write it as a story; not to use people's names, not to worry about dates and places, but just to tell the story, as if it were a novel. He said it to me several times, and finally, I got the message: just tell the story.

There was a website where people took on a novel-writing project at the same time: National Novel Writing Month, or NanoWrimo. You signed up, and committed to writing a novel of at least 50,000 words in thirty days, the thirty days of November. There was no prize, or rather, if you achieved the goal, you earned the right to buy a tee-shirt (you still had to buy it) commemorating your achievement. You are a winner!

The structure was meant to encourage writers, young writers, would-be writers, to just write. Stop prevaricating, stop pausing all the time to ask yourself, is it good enough? and just write. Get on with it. You can fuss around with it later. You can edit it or rewrite it all you like.

NanoWrimo started in July 1999 with twenty-one participants in San Francisco. In 2022 there were 413,00 participants all around the world. But it ended its life in March 2025 because of philosophical disagreements about the use of artificial intelligence.

Although I did not commune much with the other people who were writing a book, it gave me some satisfaction to put up a page on the website and track my progress. But, could I do it? It was so long ago. I had some records and relics of the job in my filing cabinet, but I understood, I was not to rely on that.

I had been the manager of an organisation that provided disability services, and after five productive years, a group of people moved in who were corrupt and self-serving. It ended in my getting the sack. But when I took a story approach, it was not dry facts, it was a drama. And that's how I had lived it.

As I sat there in front of the computer, it gradually came back to me, a story that spread over six years, beginning with the president who was arrested at the end of my first week for stealing all of the organisation's funds. I was able to write from day to day, filling out the shape of the story, from its opening disaster to its emerging health and growth, and the emergence of the unsavoury people, all the way to the ugly conclusion.

It all came back. Once I had started, it poured out: 63,000 words in 30 days. It became my first "novel": *The Ten Thousand Things*. It was immensely satisfying, even cathartic. It also gave me satisfaction to buy the tee-shirt. Over the years, I did this exercise several times.

One of the ideas that percolated during that month was the idea that a distinguishing feature of writing is that it is not a performance art. It is something you have prepared beforehand and perfected to your satisfaction before anyone sees it. A singer or a dancer performs on the spot, in front of the audience. This is the essential difference.

I was fearful about performing on the spot. That was a big reason why I did not want to be a singer or a dancer, and I was drawn to writing. I suppose that the singer and the dancer are mostly enacting rehearsed pieces, and a writer is creating something from a blank page, just as the song-writer and the choreographer are before their work is taken to the stage.

However, the common ideal is of being able to speak or dance spontaneously in front of the audience. What NanoWrimo did for me was to offer a context, a type of stage, where you could not go back. You had to keep moving forward. There was no time to revise; you had to keep writing the story each day. Later, you could review and adjust things, but for thirty days you had to keep moving. There was no room to doubt yourself.

You are swept along, you have to involve yourself in the story and go with it. You may have had a good plan, but it can go awry. Sometimes the characters don't play nice. Some of them have issues you didn't know about, and they want to air them at inconvenient moments.

And of course, all of them want to distract you with something that's important to them. They tug mightily in their own direction. You have to know when to follow them and when to resist them. You have to be the maestro. And all the time, it's not so much them that is being revealed but you, the author. That's the shocking thing.

The one who wants to be a writer, I learned, is beguiled by the thought that they are invisible, that they do not have to dance on stage in person. People do not have to see your feet, watch your posture, hear your voice. You are behind a veil, pulling the strings. You are not really present; you are at a distance. You are safe.

I found that these are all illusions. This was so even when I was telling a true story. I did not learn all of this the first year, but each time I did NanoWrimo, something new would come up and challenge me. I had to remember, the point of the story is to tell the story without getting in the way of it. And the way to do this is to be doubtless, to forget about the fact that you are on show, and just tell the story.

And I realise now, that the word "author" and the word "authentic" come from the same root.

Suddenly, I had another book to publish. This was still in the days when the best option for people like me was a small print run. But a small print run was considered to be 1,000 books. If you were serious, you organised a print run in China and ordered at least 5,000 copies. But I was a writer, not a business person, and not a book marketer.

I did the "small" print run, and I organised a book launch at a bookshop. I asked three people to speak about the book for me. It was a successful event; over fifty people attended, and I sold enough books to cover the costs of the event. However, there was no residual effect. The bookshop was not interested in taking the books to sell.

I discovered that most bookshops will not take books from an individual; you have to be a book company, such as a publisher or distributor. The other factor was that we were now in the years when book distributors were failing because of the effect of the internet, and online booksellers were expanding. I offered books for sale on my website, but not many people found my website.

However, before long there was a new phenomenon: print-on-demand books. Instead of printing a large (to me) pile of books and filling my garage with them, I could print one, or ten, or a hundred. This changed the rules entirely. Could I now devise a new career plan as a writer?

I think this development did make a change for me. It meant that I could publish books without filling up the garage with boxes and boxes of books. If this development had not occurred, I would have probably allowed wisdom to prevail and stopped writing books. It would have been the sensible course of action.

It meant that I could glance out again at the shape of my life and include writing in it. I had spent long enough writing for other people, I did not want to spend another decade or two as a contract for hire. I still needed to work, but I was happy to do training, design of training materials, things that were related to my "practical" career.

I had spent those three hard years in my early twenties learning how to teach mathematics to a classroom of children. I had extended those skills to be able to teach many other subjects to many other groups of people. I had acquired my Master of Education degree and I understood what I was doing as a designer of training as well. I had also applied my skills to the field of business ethics.

I no longer felt that teaching was simply a safe occupation for me, and one that avoided taking on the real career of writing. Why? It was because of this: to say that one is a writer is to say very little. The important question is the next one: what do you write? One may write romance novels or westerns, one may write police reports from the daily beat, one may write shopping lists, or letters to local politicians (or for local politicians).

This perspective was important at this time, because I had started a new area of study: family history. My mother had turned ninety, and at the lunch for her birthday, I looked around and realised that I could not name with certainty all of her brothers and sisters, and that statement was even more true of my father's brothers and sisters.

Beyond this, I knew nothing of either of their parents. And this seemed a silly state of affairs. It should be possible to find out all of this. My mother was of some help, although in certain areas she was guarded. But it was a challenge, and I was ready to take it on. Gradually, my knowledge grew. I could construct a family tree and I was building an extensive online repository of information.

Some of the stories were surprising, and remarkable. Some of them were deeply sad. At a certain point, I realised that all of this knowledge was not accessible to anyone else. I tried to be organised, but it still needs to be represented as a story in order for it to be accessible. I realised that I would have to figure out what I wanted to write down about this whole new adventure. I had children and grandchildren to consider, because they had a right to know too, and many of the stories were of wider significance as well.

The search itself was also of interest, at least to me, and the first book I wrote was called *A Modest Quest*. It was an ironic title, admitting that in family history, there is no such thing as a modest quest; one discovery leads onto the next, and to the need to discover what came before that. The people all come alive again. After this, I wrote several more books on family history. Some focused on particular people, one dealt with how all of my direct ancestors migrated to Australia, another two books consisted of shorter stories.

There are still numerous subjects that wait for me to address them. Generally, this means that a person is in need of explanation. One person was a bigamist. I discovered him because I wondered about my father's first wife, who had died when she was about thirty. When I obtained the marriage certificate, I saw that she had also been married before, and although she was now still in her early twenties, she was a divorced petitioner. I wondered about that.

After I found her first marriage certificate, I unearthed the story. The husband had been a bigamist; he had actually been married to two women previously: a trigamist? He was charged with bigamy and he ended up going to gaol. But there was more after that, so the story needs to be told, and I have to dive into it all again so that I can understand what sort of man he was.

In recent years, I have found that my reflective stories have come to include elements of family history. It seems inescapable. My reflective stories have become travel stories, or vice versa. There was *Travel with a Pen*, and *The Quilt Approach: A Tasmanian Patchwork*. Most recently there was *The Traveller, Lost*. All of these books incorporate family history, because that's what I do when I travel: I explore the many different places in the history of the people in my big family.

Given that I am now in the years that are called retirement, I have as much time as I want to be a writer, which also entails being a researcher and a thinker. I have reached the point where people no longer ask you what your career plan is. Of course, there is the retrospective question: what was your career?

Perversely, I did have the thought when I turned sixty-five, that I had made it to this point without having a career plan. I had done it!

My good fortune is that there is no division between my life and my work. For many people, it is not like this. If you have been the driver of a freight train, you can no longer do that. But there are some jobs where you can continue to exercise your skills in a hobbyist manner. A mechanic can still be a mechanic in his backyard, and a teacher can find a place to exercise teacher-skills. My mother did dressmaking jobs well into her eighties.

I get up in the morning and add another sentence to the piece I was working on yesterday. A missing word occurred to me in the middle of the night.

PART 3: WAYS OF NOT HAVING A CAREER PLAN

Chapter 11: Fundamentals of career planning

I have talked to many people about this book's title: the importance of not having a career plan. Invariably they like it, but why?

They say things like this:

- I never had a normal career. I went from this thing to that thing to another thing, and I didn't think that was a bad thing.
- We were told that the career path is a ladder. You choose what to do, then you go up the steps on that ladder: junior accountant, qualified accountant, senior accountant, manager, partner.... That only applies to a small number of people.
- Most of the movement in my career has been sideways. Very seldom have I gone straight up, Generally I have taken a horizontal move, into a different set of skills, and later on I have got a position because of my breadth of experience.
- Sometimes, a promotion into a manager role (which seems like the obvious thing to do) is a dead-end move. You discover that the work is quite menial, and often, there is no career path.

- Rather than seeking promotion, I found I was better off leaving the company and working as a contractor or consultant.

"It is a journey whose end is not yet seen. Our protagonist may eventually be ready to be the hero of his/her own life."

In Parts 1 and 2, I described the course of my life. Like some of the people I quoted above, I never had a straightforward path through life. Mostly that was due to the fact that I knew that writing was important to me, but I didn't know how to translate that into a decent living. For much of my life as well, I did not feel that I was good enough to make my own way against the mass weight of others in society. Nor did I feel that I had anything to express that people would find interesting or attractive.

One of the holy grails of this feeling is the PhD. You think, "If I had a PhD, people would respect me." I could write a book about ethics, but why would anybody buy it? But if I was Doctor Martin, that would be different. Then, people would trust that I knew what I was talking about.

There are still things I have not divulged. There was one point, after I had published the first ethics book, when I applied to a university to do a PhD in Business Ethics. I was accepted, and I began. I sketched out what I would do as the research for the PhD, and wrote a proposal that explained my methodology and the literature I would be drawing on.

However, never in twelve months did I get the feeling that my supervisor or the head of the school understood or even cared about what I was doing. It was going to be a thesis on business ethics from the values perspective I had already framed and articulated in my book. Instead, I was told it would be best to put aside what I had written in the book. I was told to pick an existing thesis that I liked, and just do a variation on it. I would get a PhD, I would achieve the goal.

It culminated in a meeting (after many months) where I laid out my proposal and explained the steps I would be taking to achieve it, and the only response I got was, "There is no schedule included in your document." There was no comment on my proposal at all. I had had enough. I stormed out, and they requested my resignation the same week, which I was very glad to submit to them.

After that experience, I questioned the relevance of being able to say that I am Doctor Martin, if that meant I stood on top of a mountain consisting of people and institutions like that. I am better off being non-affiliated. I am not Doctor Martin.

The important thing is to be clear about what you are talking or writing about, to understand it well, and to be able to relate it to people's concerns.

What is your career goal? One must have a goal before one can formulate a plan.

It may be fair to say that most people do not rise above mediocrity. And why is that? Part of it is that most people fear being different. They fear standing out from the crowd. Allied with this is the illusion that in the crowd, one is safe and secure. This is followed by the fear of success.

Accordingly, the shared feeling of mediocrity creates conformity, which is self-reinforcing. It becomes its own authority.

Against this is the idea of breaking out of mediocrity, of rebelling, of becoming "who you really are" as an individual. This is to carve your own path, not following others, or trends. The idea behind this is that it is natural, that being spontaneous leads to a natural flowering, to the fulfilment of your potential. It requires that you don't rely on what others think.

There is a joy in the creative process. It is to manifest a dream rather than to simply have the dream. This applies to creators, whether they are artistic enterprises or professions and trades, and it likewise applies to managers and leaders. One must distinguish oneself from mediocrity.

It is not as if one ignores other people. Rather, it is that one knows what is for the good of all, that one can see what meets people's needs, what helps them. One does not simply accept what is; one considers what one can do to improve matters.

There is that story about a stonemason working at a church, and someone asks him what he is doing. He says, "I am laying stones, one on top of the other." Another stonemason answers differently. He says, "I am building the archway for the entrance to the church", while yet another has a third answer: "I am contributing to making something beautiful for God." Or he might simply say, "I am creating something beautiful."

You can see what is being presented here. You can just focus on the immediate work, and carry out the steps unthinkingly. At another level, you can see the work in its wider context: it is part of something meaningful that a group of humans is doing together. And at the third level, the work is about the workman fulfilling his capacities and serving the good of all.

So, the beginning of career planning lies in knowing what the important things in life are. I say there are four things:

- Competence
- Morality
- Beauty
- Love.

With the three stonemasons, you can see some of this. They are all interested in competency. The second stonemason subscribes to an extended version of competency, a wider vision of what the work is. And the third stonemason believes in beauty as well.

We hope that they all subscribe to morality. And what about love? There is no question with the third stonemason: he gives himself fully to his work. He loves what he does. On the other hand, the first stonemason holds back; he gives what he must, and no more. The second stonemason is in between.

This is a way to look at your work life. Can you see the place of competency in your work: what it is, and what you would like it to be, and the place of morality, beauty and love? This is something to ponder.

Career planning explained

From this beginning, the central idea of career planning is that there is somewhere else that you want to get to, somewhere that is not here. First of all, we have to recognise that this stands in contrast to the idea that the present is sufficient and that one should enjoy it in itself. And we can ask, how does this apply to learning? Does it mean that to learn is also to not enjoy the present?

One learns because there is some knowledge, or a skill, that one wants to acquire through one's present activity. It is a conundrum: how does one enjoy the present and yet also prepare the way to one's desired future? The answer is this: that the conscious, full enjoyment of the present changes the present. Here is an example.

Suppose one wants to express something well, say, to express clearly the problems you have been having with another person. You sit down and you write about it for ten minutes. Then you leave it. The next morning, you take a fresh sheet of paper, and you write about it again. You will discover that it is not the same thing. You address the same issue, and you do it freshly, but what you write changes.

You might do this for five days. It keeps changing. And you change. At the end, you might do something in relation to the person, say, contacting them, talking to them to say something. Or you might not feel that you need to. It is enough that it has become clearer.

When our thoughts have come from sincerity, with the desire to find peace and completion, they go out into the universe as the expression of the Tao. What is the Tao? It is a concept from ancient Chinese philosophy. It can be expressed in many ways. The Tao is the breathing heart of all-that-is, the oneness, the essence, where all things come into union. It is known by the devoted, the ones who are at peace.

We start by investing in simple things, in ways of learning.

To begin again, why is there career planning?

Career planning arises because life is an adventure, and in living it, we wish to make the most of our capacities. We wish to use the capacities that we have developed to meet challenges and seize opportunities, or to do something entirely new, so that we can share in the bounty of the earth. And we recognise that this is not something done with abandon. Life has its natural laws, and our task is to find the way to act in accord with these laws in the achievement of our purposes.

And we learn not to believe anyone who claims it is otherwise, who claims that all of the earth is theirs to take if they have the strength or guile to take it. Life is inherently moral, and we should recognise that. We need to recognise that if we are to achieve something worthy and lasting.

We can talk about career planning rather than a career plan. This means that we see it as an active, ongoing function, not as the creation of a fixed thing. It means seeing our life simultaneously from two perspectives:

- Living actively now, fulfilling what is required of the current situation with our best efforts, and
- Having a future perspective, with which we see where our current work and situation could lead to.

The future perspective means that we will move into expanding capability. We will increasingly utilise our talents and pursue our interests, rather than having to suppress them in order to make a living. Moreover, as well as earning a living, we will contribute something worthwhile to the world.

"The meaning of life is to find your gift. The purpose of life is to give it away." – Pablo Picasso

Career planning, to be purposeful, needs to have a vision of what it involves and where it heads. The diagram below tries to illustrate this. The overview is that we need two perspectives: who am I? and what is the context in which I operate? (the latter could be an organisation that employs you, or it could be the marketplace if you are an independent agent.)

There is an intersection between oneself and one's context. We need to know what this is. One studies both. There is one set of activities that is our self-assessment. Complementing this is a set of activities that is our environmental assessment.

From our study of both these aspects, we devise an Action Plan. What are our preferred work roles? In pursuance of this, what are our learning goals? How do we market ourselves in the world? And how do we conduct a search for suitable jobs?

This process is repeated at intervals. We return to it as our situation changes and we change.

Figure 1: Career Planning Process

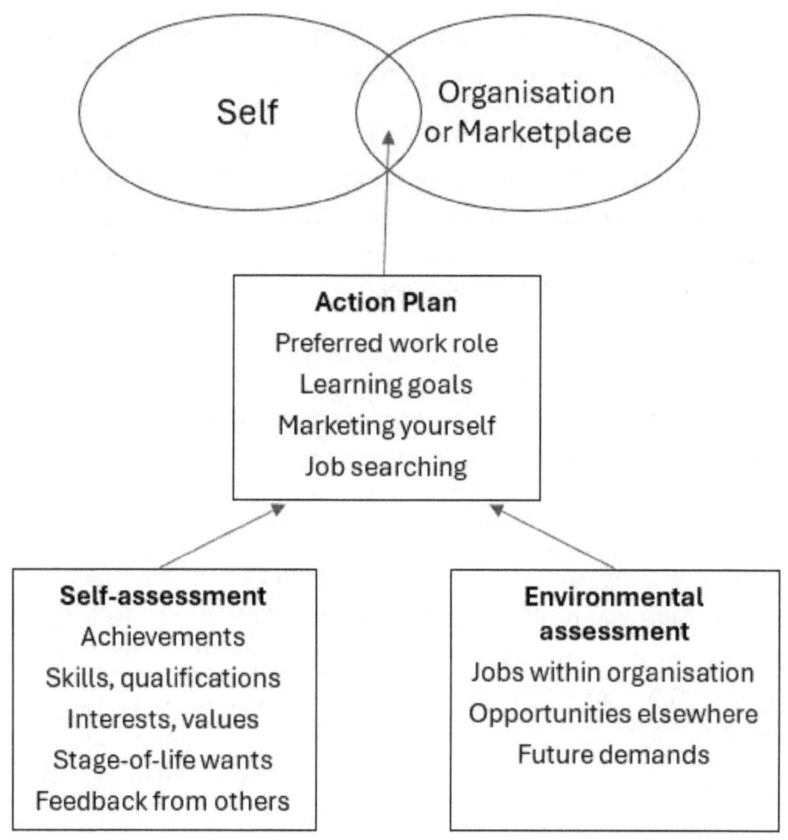

The environment for jobs (and work)

Career development may now include a number of alternative types of movement, rather than simple progression up a corporate ladder. Possible career directions include:

- **Vertical** – traditional promotion
- **Enrichment** – improving skills and adding skills

• **Lateral** – change of job or change of direction

• **Exploratory** – looking around, investigating choices, looking for variety of work, including part-time work

• **Realignment** – making a new start, going back to basics, including drops in position and salary

• **Relocation** – new start in new firm or new location.

It helps to be able to see yourself in your environment. This is where you start to get ideas as to what direction you can move in, and where you want to move.

For employees, the first place to look is the other possibilities within the organisation. Secondly, one looks at opportunities elsewhere. Thirdly, you need to look to the future: what kinds of jobs are likely to open up, and what jobs will atrophy?

Self-assessment

As the diagram shows, self-assessment starts with listing tangible aspects of yourself:

- What are your qualifications and skills?
- What are your interests and values?
- What are your achievements?
- What do you need and want at this stage of your life?
- Feedback from others: what do others think about your strengths (and weaknesses)?

You may not have written all of this down before, and doing so may enable you to think differently about yourself.

Action Plan

In devising an action plan, you have in mind what you have just explored: yourself and your environment. Then, you think of your career goals: what would your preferred work role be?

Having clarified this, you need to think about:

- Your learning goals
- How to market yourself
- What job searching to do.

Always, it is a question of "who am I?" and "who do I want to be?" in the world you inhabit. Your expression of this might even include the thought: "How would I like to make the world a better place?"

There is much more that can be said. As the world becomes more complex and fast-changing, one needs to think about career development competencies. We have qualifications and skills in a particular work area, but nowadays we need to develop competencies in the very process of career development.

Career development competencies

If you are to take a conscious approach to your career, you should think about the following competencies. There are three groups of them:

- how you manage yourself
- how you undertake ongoing learning
- how you focus particularly on career-building actions and activities.

These can be spelled out in more detail. It is best to consider how you measure up against each item. For example, you might choose one that you feel unsure about, and focus on that for a week, asking yourself, how could I do this better?

Some of these things are more tangible than others. For example, how do you "build and maintain a positive self-image"? This is simply saying to trust yourself and who you are. In one sense, it takes a lifetime of learning. In another sense, you can start now, observing your positive qualities, and trusting that you have a right to be here and you have something to give.

Area A: Personal management

1. Build and maintain a positive self-concept.

2. Interact positively and effectively with others.

3. Change and grow throughout your life.

Area B: Ongoing learning

4. Participate in ongoing learning that is supportive of your career goals.

5. Obtain relevant information about your career direction.

6. Improve your understanding of the relationship between work, society and the economy.

Area C: Career building

7. Obtain or create, and maintain, work that remunerates you appropriately.

8. Make work decisions that are career-enhancing.

9. Maintain a healthy balance between your work and your other roles in life.

10. Understand the changing nature of work roles.

11. Improve how you understand the career-building process.

This account covers a lot of territory. Is it overwhelming? And how does it relate to the particular environment in which you find yourself?

We need to come back out to the wider view. We can say there are three tiers of skills or qualities involved in career development:

- Tier 1: Foundational capabilities – the skills that people generally need in any job; these include personal skills, interpersonal skills, and business and management skills
- Tier 2: Job-specific capabilities – the skills and knowledge people need in your specific job/occupation
- Tier 3: Future career direction – skills related to the future; these include career development skills, skills related to management and leadership, and skills that are currently emerging in the workforce.

Figure 2: A Career Framework for Professionals

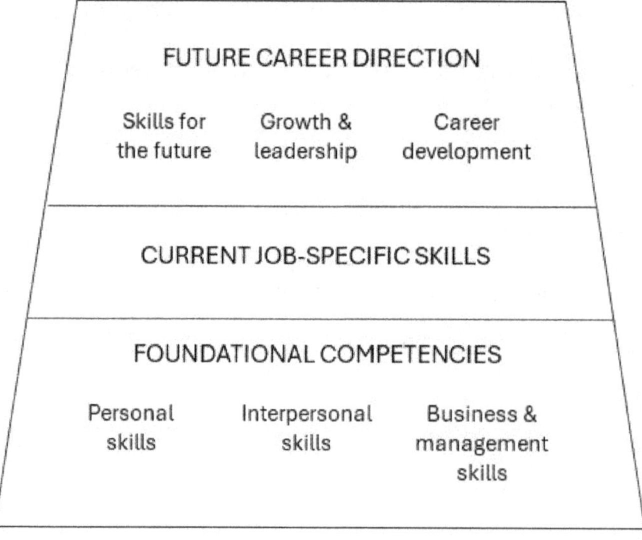

The lists of competencies in each of these areas are shown below. It may seem too much, but in reading the lists, one may find that there are one or more items that you haven't thought about much, and maybe it is important, and you could give it some attention.

Tier 1: Foundational capabilities

Area A: Personal skills

- Self-management and autonomy
- Problem-solving
- Initiative and enterprise
- Achieving performance outcomes
- Continuous learning and development
- Ethics and values
- Adaptability.

Area B: Interpersonal skills

- Verbal communication
- Written communication
- Teamwork and collaboration
- Relationship-building
- Influencing skills
- Working with diversity and culture.

Area C: Business and management skills

- Technology skills
- Knowledge of the business context
- Knowledge of the organisation and its strategies and policies
- Planning, organising and implementing actions
- Analysing needs and proposing solutions
- Focus on clients
- Core skills: language, literacy, numeracy
- Safety, environmental and sustainability skills.

Tier 2: Job-specific capabilities

The content of this section depends on the kind of job, profession or occupation it is.

- Comprehensive, coherent knowledge of the job
- Competence in relevant skills
- Ability to apply knowledge in context
- Understanding of connections to other job areas and work roles
- Demonstrated ethical values and integrity
- Responsible engagement in work and civic life
- Respect for diversity and social justice principles
- Positive contribution to sustainable change.

Tier 3: Future career direction

Area A: Career development competencies

These are the skills described above. Future career direction refers to where they fit into the bigger picture.

Area B: Skills related to management and leadership

- Strategic thinking
- Vision, inspiration, being able to articulate it
- Ability to deal with complexity and ambiguity
- Energy and drive
- Political astuteness
- Steadfastness, ethics, integrity, self-control
- Social character: awareness of personal and cultural differences, respect, compassion
- Organisational and tactical skills
- Culture-building, leading change and learning.

Area C: Future and emerging skills

- Sense-making and critical thinking
- Social intelligence
- Novel and adaptive thinking
- Cross-cultural competency
- Computational thinking
- New media literacy
- Understanding of concepts across disciplines
- Design mindset
- Cognitive load management
- Virtual collaboration.

Finding focus

The wide view shows us the complexity of humans and the breadth of their work and their involvements. How should we respond to it? The answer may be to decrease our involvements, rather than increasing them. This is what makes energy available for new developments.

Can you impose a direction on things? Can you make any helpful resolutions? Can you maintain your resolve? To do this, you have to keep examining yourself. What are your motivations? Sometimes an outer limit on our circumstances forces our inner development. We clarify our purpose.

Keep asking, what is helpful in my situation and what is not? How quickly can you let go of things that are not helpful? One author says, "Once a goal has been selected, nothing else must interfere. Cut out all that is ordinarily considered essential in order to find meaning."

As Picasso said, "The meaning of life is to find your gift."

But Picasso also challenges us. He goes on to say, "The purpose of life is to give our gift away." Are these puzzling words?

I take it to mean we should be using our gift, we should be sharing it, we should be developing it and refining it. We may need to adapt the gift to our circumstances, as I felt I was doing when I was a manager. Writing is part of foundational capabilities. It was also part of the job-specific skills, and it was an expression of leadership skills.

There is also, in Picasso's words, the whiff of spontaneity: give your gift away. As you focus on the development of your gift, you develop reserves of power and grace. You activate creative power, you adapt to circumstances and find the place for the new. You can respond freely when the time comes.

Fuzzy goals

There is another thing to be said, because often our thinking goes haywire because of pre-conceived notions we have. The idea of "goals" sounds very precise, so we might go astray by trying to establish a goal that is very clear, when in fact it is too difficult at the point where you are at the moment. At times, it might be better to have a "fuzzy goal". What could that be?

Commonly, goals apply to industrial, repetitive contexts where we want predictable, consistent results. But in some spheres, for example, creative work, we are not looking for predictability, but for breakthrough ideas. We don't want to incrementally improve things, we want to generate something new.

In this context, the important skill is to find the correct questions to ask. Some people talk about having a "pole-star vision" which motivates the general direction of work without blinding the person to opportunities along the way. The goal is not vague as to be unable to be described at all; it must give people a sense of purpose while leaving them room to follow their intuition.

The pathway may be ambiguous, uncertain and complex. There are many unknowns and there are no examples to follow, and there are risks of failure. It may not be easy to define. For example, one does not write a novel by saying how many words it will consist of.

One image is this: the fuzzy goal is like a far-off planet. We won't know what it really looks like until we get closer. The guide is to start with something that is as fuzzy as it needs to be.

One also needs to think about: when you achieve your goal, will you be able to recognise it? One writer says that achieving a fuzzy goal is as much about developing a better understanding of the goal as it is about the achievement of the goal.

Another image is about climbing a mountain: you know broadly where you want to get to, but you don't know what you will encounter along the way. In this sense the goal is fuzzy.

The fuzziness of the goal also means that you have to make frequent stops to reassess the changing situation based on what you have experienced and what you have learned. Think back to the industrial metaphor and think about what is different from that.

In moving towards a fuzzy goal, one has to monitor one's emotions and motivation, because the point of a career goal is that you arrive at something that you find fulfilling.

In moving towards a fuzzy goal, you also have to regularly assess whether you are moving towards the goal or away from it, or stagnating. It may not be as easy as assessing whether you are getting closer to the top of the mountain.

Once again, it is important to understand that your progress is only partly about navigating terrain. It is also about continually practising self-examination and cultivating virtue. It is only in this way that you will learn when to persevere in pushing forward and when it is wiser to wait. And we also need to keep aware of the people around us. Helping a colleague is part of the journey, not something to abandon because we are intent on our own career goals.

One also needs to understand timing. There are times when all the doors are closed, and there are times when doors open. What one learns is the futility of pushing against closed doors. One should preserve one's energy at such times, not complaining, and observe when things change.

Lastly, we should remember that the journey is long, and it will not be accomplished in a day. Accordingly, "the superior person comes home towards sundown and relaxes, recovering his/her energy".

Chapter 12: Creative people without careers

What does "not planning" mean?

One of the important distinctions is between the concept of a career plan (a noun) as a fixed plan that you follow rigidly, step by step, and the concept of career planning (a verb) that can change as you go, fluidly and adaptively, while keeping alive the core that excites you.

"Not planning" can mean any of the following things:

- Being open to unusual opportunities
- Reframing your own past, seeing it from a different perspective, eg seeing skills and understandings that you hadn't articulated before
- Continuing to pursue the things that you like doing; it may even mean things that you just want to try out for a while
- Not staying in the one job for too long. What does this mean? If it feels stale, it may be time to go; you are not learning anything new, you have become the fall guy for all

the problems of the organisation, and you are not rewarded for it

- Being ready (and able) to take on bigger challenges, eg a different industry, moving a long way away
- Not rejecting a job that might look like a step backwards to other people, because it might serve a purpose for you.

"If one has a powerful motivation for living, then choices are clear-cut. With discipline, sacrifices are made for a higher goal, and one acts with confidence and directness." – Deng Ming-Dao

Rejecting the trodden path

People start out their working life in different ways. I have told the story of the chemical engineer who, after about twenty years, became a management consultant. It was a career he could not have foreseen when he was twenty. But there are other people who start out by rejecting the trodden path.

Joseph Campbell is known as the writer on mythology. During his lifetime he came to be called the world's leading exponent of mythology. He explored the deeper, internal components of myths from all over the world. He formed the view that the mythologies of cultures have an underlying pattern. His first book, in 1949, was called *The Hero with a Thousand Faces*. His ideas have become extremely popular, and have contributed to many movies and books. George Lucas said that the *Star Wars* films followed Campbell's ideas very closely.

Since then, Campbell's ideas have informed many movie studios, who came to see his ideas as a template providing a framework for compelling tales that spoke intimately to people. And yet this immense popularity only came after George Lucas's public expression of admiration for Campbell's book. For years after the Hero book was released, it was only a quiet seller.

Campbell had started his working life by rejecting the obvious pathway of academia. He was born in 1904 in New York, and at first he studied biology and mathematics. After this he switched to Arts at Columbia University, specialising first in English literature then in medieval literature. However, he wanted a much broader canvas; he wanted to add Sanskrit and modern art to his studies, and psychology and mythology. Columbia did not agree.

The view of Columbia was the accepted one. In academia, you chose a field, a narrow field, and you stuck to it. Campbell refused to choose. He resigned from his studies and went to live in the country, in a rented cabin at Woodstock, New York. It was 1929, and a month later the stock market crashed and the Great Depression began. It seemed that Campbell's decision was disastrous.

But Campbell was busy. He was reading, and he spent the next five years reading books on all the things he wanted to know. Later, he said, about his difference of opinion with the university, "A crisis forces you into truth, and the truth was, I needed to read." He was reading methodically, for nine hours a day.

After five years, Campbell came out of the woods and managed to obtain a job teaching at a girls' college, where they allowed him to teach across the breadth of material he had been imbibing. He taught there for nearly forty years. The Hero book came out in 1949; it had taken him until then to work through and synthesise all the ideas that had emerged from his intensive reading. The initial reaction was tepid and confused. But he said, "If it's true, time will reveal it."

Christopher Vogler, who wrote *The Writer's Journey* (1998), based on Campbell's ideas on mythology, said that *The Hero with a Thousand Faces* "was my atlas, a book of maps for my own writing journey". He became a story consultant at the Disney corporation based on this foundation.

As an old man, Campbell was filmed in interview with Bill Moyers for PBS and it became the most popular interview in PBS's history.

One writer, commenting on Campbell's life, said, "Sometimes, the worst career move isn't a mistake. Sometimes it's the doorway to the destiny no one else can see."

I see it a bit differently. Sometimes you yourself cannot see the doorway to destiny. I think Joseph Campbell simply had the obstinacy to stick to what his inner drive was telling him. I think Campbell's own comment is closer to the truth:

"You must give up the life you planned, in order to have the life that is waiting for you." – Joseph Campbell

It may not rain in your lifetime

Joseph Campbell is a man who remained true to his inner drive, and later in his life other people discovered what he had to say and his ideas became enormously popular. But we need to also take account of situations where this does not occur. It may still be that a person is being true to their inner drive, but the world does not give its acclaim to the person in their lifetime.

The vocations where being known widely would seem to be essential to success are writing, art and music. Yet there are many examples of people who became widely known only after their death. Think of this list of famous writers, artists and musicians:

- Vincent Van Gogh (artist)
- John Keats (poet)
- William Blake (poet and artist)
- Jane Austen (*Pride and Prejudice*)
- Emily Bronte (*Wuthering Heights*)
- Sylvia Plath (poet, author)
- Stieg Larsson (*The Girl with the Dragon Tattoo*)
- Jeff Buckley (musician)
- Eva Cassidy (singer).

The common thread? Not one of them was famous during their life. Some of them were known modestly, among small circles of people. Some of them had published in a small way. Emily Bronte, for example, had published her novel under the name "Ellis Bell". Eva Cassidy had been in the studio and recorded some songs. Sylvia Plath had published poems in magazines, and the novel *The Bell Jar* was published in the same year as her suicide in 1963. During his lifetime, only one of Van Gogh's paintings, *The Red Vineyard*, was sold.

One may ask, how important was being known to these people? I think the general answer is that all of them made some efforts for others to know their works, but it would be fair to say that none of them made a concerted effort, and none of them met with instant or runaway success. There were negative reviews of, or reservations about, their work as well, where it was known at all.

From the perspective of the creator, the message is, "Do the work," or even, "Just do the work."

To go back to Joseph Campbell, how does he fit, against these other creators? One might ask, because it was really the trigger of George Lucas that caused him to become so famous. He might just as easily have died in obscurity.

I think Joseph Campbell "did the work". He spent many, many years working to reach an understanding of a vast field of knowledge: as many cultures, ancient and modern, that he could learn about, and their mythologies, and he did the deep thinking to try and find the patterns between them all. That he became so well-known could be called an accident of history. You might say the same of Van Gogh, Keats and all the others mentioned above.

There are other thinkers who sought to articulate and integrate a broad field of knowledge too, such as Ken Wilber. Wilber also worked outside of formal academia, and established his own institute, the Integral Institute. There are many ways one can pursue the inner drive. In some cases, the work meets with acclaim and it spreads. In other cases, that does not occur. If the work is somehow found, one has to judge it on its merits, according to one's own lights.

Robert Martiensen

In Australia, there was a recent discovery of thousands of artworks painted by one man in seclusion and not known to anyone until his death. Robert Martiensen lived by himself in the countryside in South Australia, in an old farmhouse, and he had few contacts with the world. He was visited occasionally by his sister and her husband, but they never entered the house; they always spoke on the verandah.

When it was discovered that he had died, people first entered the house, discovering not only his body, but paintings stacked everywhere in the house, in every room, and a room set up for painting. There were around 7,000 paintings, large and small. Van Gogh was prolific in his output, producing over 2,000 paintings in his life. What Martiensen had done dwarfed even that.

Martiensen's work had been produced entirely in the few years since his retirement as a teacher of mathematics. Not a soul knew that he was a serious painter. His family and the few people who knew him knew that he dabbled in painting. He gave them occasional small painted pieces in thanks for favours, but these were seen as inconsequential, and they were discarded.

The family concluded that Martiensen was simply eccentric, and had no interest in the paintings. They wanted to sell the property and end their association with it, so they engaged a stock and station agent to carry out the task. When the agent came to view the house, he was stunned. He had never come across anything like this. Yes, he had a job to do, but he needed to know something about the paintings first.

There was an urgency about this time. The family wanted everything done immediately, and planned an auction. The agent moved all the paintings out of the house and into a large shed temporarily. And he found Elizabeth Arthur, a woman who had her own gallery in Victoria, and who was a valuer of paintings as well as a practising psychotherapist. She came to look at the collection, and was similarly stunned. She had likewise never seen anything like it.

They had to piece the story together. It seemed that Martiensen, on his retirement from a perfectly respectable career of teaching mathematics in South Australian country schools, had retired to the house in which he had grown up and begun an entirely new life. In the house they found stacks of books on art: modern art, the history of art, Picasso, indigenous art, Miro, Mondrian, Kandinsky, and more.

Wandering through the paintings, they saw that he had produced paintings that reflected each of these schools. They were all abstract, and the product of a mathematical mind; none of them were realist. The titles show that he had addressed his paintings to all manner of subjects: music, literature, medicine, art, mythology, mathematics, science and more.

Those first weeks were difficult for Elizabeth Arthur, because she spent periods of time when she did not know what was going on, and only she knew the urgency of the situation. When she discovered that the house had been sold, she was left to wonder what had happened to the paintings.

She discovered that they had been sold to a dealer, someone who had a collectibles bazaar. She met him, and found that his thought was to sell them off piece by piece, hoping to make a profit on his investment. She managed to persuade him to hold onto the entire collection for two years, until it could be assessed. His vision was still to sell off the pieces, but he agreed, and he remained true to his word.

Martiensen has been described as an "outsider artist" because he never tried to sell or exhibit any of his work, and he was not influenced by any kind of artistic community. His sole references were the books on art that he had bought.

As a teacher, Martiensen was described as brilliant. He was also an avid sportsman despite having one leg shorter than the other, the result of having had polio as a child. Apart from this, Elizabeth Arthur describes him as an elusive, enigmatic and eccentric intellectual.

This story is depicted in the book, *The Secret: Robert Martiensen*, by Elizabeth Arthur (2020).

How would we describe him in terms of careers? I can relate to him (apart from his having been a teacher of mathematics) because he took one of the routes that I consider to be acceptable in life: he found a skilled occupation in which he could earn a living, one that gave him some satisfaction in the exercise of that skill and proficiency. But, it is profoundly evident that he did not lose that inner drive. Given the eventual opportunity, he threw himself into the work, studying the previous practitioners, and considering what he would like to do in the face of their work.

Elizabeth Arthur raises the question of whether Martiensen had psychiatric problems. That is as may be. A better question may be this: how would Martiensen himself have measured his progression in his artistic career?

Perhaps we could apply the items above about job-specific qualities:

- Comprehensive, coherent knowledge of the job
- Competence in relevant skills
- Ability to apply knowledge in context

- Understanding of connections to other job areas and work roles
- Demonstrated ethical values and integrity
- Responsible engagement in work and civic life
- Respect for diversity and social justice principles
- Positive contribution to sustainable change.

Given his intense and persistent focus, and the fact that he created an immense body of work, which I would say is also coherent, I would accept his dedication to his "career".

Another question that arises is, did he ever intend to exhibit his work? There is no evidence that he did. So, had he just resigned himself to the current work, to keep going faithfully? He seemed to have no plan for anything beyond the work of producing more and more expressions of the inner drive he felt.

Do we come now with criticism? Do we say that it would have been better if he had found a way to balance out his life? Artists generally have periods of production interspersed with times when they exhibit their work, and talk about it with people. (There is usually a financial reason for this too. One sells one's work and gets paid for it, and this contributes to living, and to the purchase of more materials for future works.)

In Martiensen's case we have accept that we are faced with a phenomenon, the huge output of a man who had an inner drive of great energy, that fired his imagination in multiple directions. If we were talking about someone contemporary, we might well consider all the above qualities and encourage the person to be more accessible, to share their gift, thinking of the words of Picasso.

There is another aspect of this story too: Elizabeth Arthur. Here was a woman who had a successful career, in fact, two careers: psychotherapist and art valuer. But when she came upon Martiensen's work, she was faced with a decision: was she going to take on responsibility for his enormous body of work, initially fighting to preserve it, and then assessing its meaning and value?

It was clearly going to be a huge project. Why did she not simply say, I already have a career, and back away from it? I have tried to make the point that, in determining one's career, one must make moral choices, and one must look for work that is for the well-being of all. A corollary of this is that in the midst of your career, you may be faced with choices that demand your action, in the interests of the well-being of all.

The legacy of Martiensen was that he had created a huge body of work that reflected many of the manifestations of modern art, a body of work that had been pursued without interruption or distraction, and it deserved to be recognised and understood. Its scope was such that it was relevant to the entire culture in which he had lived, say, all of Australia and indeed, all of the world.

To Ellizabeth Arthur's credit, she changed her life around to make room for the project, and followed through with the work it entailed.

This is what it might mean not to have a career plan.

Practise self-examination and cultivate virtue. Continue to strengthen your character.

Richard Lockwood

I remember one night when I was young (it was 1969 or 1970), when I rode my motorbike to Kensington to see a concert by the ebullient and enigmatic group, Tully. It turned out to be a rare event, as Tully only lasted a couple of years, splitting up in 1972. It was one of the most extraordinary concerts I had been to. It was in the Roundhouse at the University of New South Wales. It is a round building, the stage was only low, and there were no seats. People sat everywhere on the floor. The concert went for about three hours.

The music was alternatively wild and strident, then serene and soaring. It went far beyond any categories of music I was familiar with. I felt as if it was undoing categories and making something new and beautiful. After this, I did acquire an album of theirs, self-titled. But then, Tully broke up and I never heard of them again.

I had heard that they were initially the band behind the stage musical "Hair" in Sydney, but they had been sacked because they wouldn't stick to the script. They soared off on their own innovations and explorations like unruly jazz musicians.

It wasn't until recent years that I encountered Richard Lockwood, the one who had been the lead singer and multi-instrumentalist in the band. He played saxophone, flute and clarinet. He had died in 2012, and some people who knew him assembled around thirty of his songs for a double CD. On the album be plays all sorts of other instruments as well.

The songs come from over a period of forty years. After Tully broke up, essentially, he went home. It was not depression. Rather, it was the reverse: it was bliss. While he was in Tully, he had come across the holy man Meher Baba and had found joy and understanding. In his words, "I ran into a wall of light. Its brightness blinded me to all but itself and its bliss robbed me of reason for a while…. yet certitude of the formless being of Eternal Beauty and Its contemporary Personification as Avatar Meher Baba was etched onto the mirror of my soul."

A commentator of the time, John Clare, concluded, "he renounced drugs and moved through various soft and simple folky projects in which he played flute and piano, getting softer and simpler until he faded right out of music." Richard's perception of what changed is this: "eventually I side-stepped the spotlight and bowed out of the big top of public performance."

The person who compiled the collection of songs just before he died had this to say of it: "We discovered that the very private songwriter had never stopped recording after the end of his much-loved band, only that he had lost interest in making his beautiful, transcendental music available to others. *In The Doorway of the Dawn* is a revelation, the life's work of a rare talent, even rarer for his lack of concern with public recognition."

We have become so obsessed with material success in our culture that stories like that of Richard Lockwood have become both rare and unfathomable. Yet, what are we to say of it as a story about a career? He had early success. He was part of the music scene, he knew what was possible. During that time, he even went on a tour to Japan. Something changed. What was it? It was that he had an experience subsequent to which he did not need an audience to validate his songs. He was making songs for Meher Baba (the personification of love and beauty), and that was enough.

The compiler of the songs collection in 2012 expressed it this way: "He was content merely to write them, sing them, sometimes record them, offer them to his Beloved Meher Baba and then put them away in a box of cassettes in his cupboard."

This is not something one can argue with. It might make us rethink, however, what we look for in our performance of work in life. Do we need an audience to validate us? Or, do we derive joy from performing a work or exhibiting a work for an audience, joy in seeing people's gladness and engagement? It seems to be different for different people.

I think of my neighbour in the country who made high-class period-reproduction furniture. As time went on, his satisfaction was more his own, his satisfaction with the work itself. Earlier on, I think much of his satisfaction was in the worldly aspects of his work: being paid well for a piece or a collection, and the satisfaction of his clients with the new furniture for their house.

One asks, what is changing? One asks, what lasts?

One writer says, the ultimate goal is "to return to the source satisfied that you've completed your life on earth. Nothing will pull you back then. You are free."

Chapter 13: Careers and mythology

The word 'vocation' comes from a Latin root which means 'to call', and it reflects the sense of an inner calling or meaningful task which must be accomplished in the world. Although a vocation does not necessarily involve a recognised profession or the accruing of money, it needs to involve the heart in order for us to feel we have really found our place in life. It also needs to be manifested outwardly for us to feel we have achieved what we were put on earth for.

Liz Greene and Juliet Sharman-Burke, *The Mythic Journey*, Simon & Schuster, Sydney, 1999, p. 178.

The idea of a career leads to the idea that careers take a path through life that can be described, and seen in terms of a mythological journey. A career may contain trials and paradoxes. It may present us with dilemmas, and it may show us that life has deeper meaning, beyond rational thinking and cause-and-effect. Along the way, we find desire, talent, beauty, power, obstacles, suffering, loneliness, failure and triumph. The point of mythology is to help us to make sense of our lives, and to show us that we are not alone in our struggles.

The idea of mythology also reminds us that our thinking about our career is not disconnected from the story of our lives. It is part and parcel of our experience of life and our involvement in relationships.

We begin in a family. Our first awareness and our first entanglements come with our family: our parents, siblings and childhood friends, in all the variations in which these occur. We find ourselves in a particular context, with a particular family story and a particular past, which is our inheritance.

From this beginning, we have to find ourselves as an individual in the world. We leave home, we fight for our autonomy, we launch ourselves on our quest for meaning. We face relationships: passion, rejection, conflict and commitments. We seek a vocation, and struggle with ambition, greed, power and responsibility.

Along this path, we encounter rites of passage, which may involve separation, loss and suffering. There may be redemption, peace and harmony, recognition, and in the midst of these vicissitudes we may find ourselves looking at the deeper meaning of our life. And there is an end to it, where perhaps the boat will cruise to the dock peacefully.

Wouldn't you want your career to be seen this way?

The mythological perspective has been called "the hero's journey", and this might elicit criticism. Does this mean that we are talking solely about men, and does it mean that the tendency is towards militarism: the hero is a warrior? But the hero may also be a heroine, and the quest may be that of the pilgrim, the pacifist, the mother, the inventor, the adventurer or the hermit. In a career, all creative avenues are possible.

One might also ask if it is necessary that one be heroic? Historically, a hero was a demi-god with superhuman powers and courage, and similarly for a heroine. However, it should be noted that a hero or heroine also means "the principal character in a story". We should certainly accept ourselves in that sense: we are the principal character in our own story. We should not deny or refuse it.

This is not to say that the hero or heroine's journey is formulaic. Every story is different. One cannot plan out the journey. It is only evident in retrospect, which is why one needs to have courage and conviction, to go forward without knowing the end, knowing only what is true.

We also need to be deeply honest with ourselves, and recognise that, ultimately, life will demand that we be honest with our deeper callings. There are stories of people who have had motor vehicle accidents, for example, and have seen, in retrospect, that they were being woken up to what they should be doing in their life. They needed to change direction in order to move towards the expression of their innate talent that was being swamped by a job that was inappropriate.

Our journey needs to be responsive. The motor vehicle accident may mean that we go in another, unanticipated direction, and the challenges thrown up there will be different from what we were in the midst of before. Our choices need to respond to the new circumstances, and they need to do so in faithfulness to the calling, in greater recognition and acceptance of it, or else we will keep being reminded.

Let's go through the stages of the hero's (and heroine's) journey.

Stages of the journey

The ordinary world

We begin in the ordinary world. The journey takes place in its own atmosphere, but we start at home, in the circumstances where we grew up. We have discussed this before. Home may mean the parents who want you to be a success at the same occupation that one of the parents has, or it may mean the parents' best wishes for you to do whatever you want.

It may mean the child having their own unique idea (who knows why?) of what they want to be, such as the boy, the son of dairy farmers, who told his parents at a very early age that he wanted to be a barrister. The parents did not know what a barrister was, and perhaps the boy didn't have much idea either, but when the boy grew up, he went into law (happily).

The call to adventure

With careers, the call to adventure is inevitable. We grow up and we have to become something, unless we are the child of very rich parents who allow us to idle our time away. And yet, even here, the call to adventure hovers around us. There may even be a precipitating event. In my case, my father died in my final year of high school. Whilst my mother was able to keep us at school, it increased the urgency of finding an occupation as promptly as possible.

The threat in these circumstances is that we will end up in a dire or uncertain place and be trapped there forever, with no escape. Conversely, there is a promise that one will find fulfilment and ample reward in responding to the call.

At this stage, the stakes are made clear. There is a treasure to be won, there is a rebalancing of the world, there is a dream to be achieved. There may even be a challenge to be confronted. And certainty is not granted. There is the possibility that one may fail.

Refusal of the call

Given the possibility of failure, the hero faces fear, and may react in various ways to the fear. The hero may refuse the call, choosing another option. In my case, I accepted teaching as an interim occupation, having refused journalism, but I refused to make a long-term commitment to teaching.

The turning point for me was many years and many adventures later, when I saw the advertisement for a writer in Sydney, and I had been preparing myself to leave my country home for three years. Without that preparation, I would not have even noticed the job in the newspaper, or I would have not have thought that it applied to me.

The mentor (wise man, wise woman)

A wise man or woman will appear at some point, who will be father-like or mother-like towards the hero. They will encourage us. They may chastise us. They may only make a momentary appearance in our life, or they may appear and reappear at unexpected times. I think of Gandalf in *Lord of the Rings.*

In my case, I think there were various people who served this purpose temporarily over time. I also think that my mentors included the writers of the books I read, and the ideas I got from them. I could name dozens of these writers, from both fiction and non-fiction: J.R.R. Tolkien, Ursula le Guin, C.H. Dodd, Jacques Ellul, Theodor Roszak, William Irwin Thompson, W.B. Yeats, Tom Robbins, Ken Kesey. It is a long list.

An alternative perspective is given by Richard Lockwood, for whom you could say his mentor was Meher Baba. Even Robert Martiensen, grumpy and private though he was, spent some time with a painter learning techniques that he later used.

And, a mentor is only a mentor. The hero must face the challenges alone. They must even articulate the challenges for themselves.

Crossing the threshold

The threshold is the turning point between Act One and Act Two. It is where the action gets underway. The hero commits to the adventure. You can even say, "Now, there is no turning back." The problem is faced.

I had moments when I felt I was crossing a threshold. When I was at the Catholic school and I was given the task of preparing a book for the programs we were delivering, I felt that I was taking on this task as a writer. Sure, it was a pre-structured task, and I was not walking away from teaching right at the moment, but it was a shift in my mind. Later, opportunities came my way, like the project to write the history of the shire in which I lived.

Challenges and tests, allies and enemies

The world that the hero enters into has its own characteristics and its own rules. In the movies it could be a sleazy bar, and some of the people in it are villains. It could be a corporate office where there is a hierarchy, everyone has their own behavioural idiosyncrasies, and the place itself has its own secret rules. You may be bewildered or humiliated until you learn how to claim your space, how to harness respect.

In these places, our character is tested. We are learning how to react under stress.

It is here that we might start to appreciate what it means to be a hero in an adventure. We might have been expecting things to be easier or more polite. The trouble is that some of the other people are playing a part in their own adventure. A salutary case was when I was the manager and the man from the committee insinuated that he could make things easier for me (with the implication that he could make them tougher as well). My first instinct was to treat it as a joke, but fortunately, just as quickly I realised it was important to treat it like a scene in a sleazy bar, and I had to be tougher than him.

The cave: the innermost place of danger

In the myths, eventually there is a place where something critical will take place. It is the darkest place, where death may occur. Less dramatically, in a career, it is a meeting or event where you face a situation that is critical for your advance or stagnation.

It is a proving time where we stand on our merit or fall short. In my story there were several of these points. Some of them you could even count as losses, but they were not; they were times when I did what I needed to do. One was the time when I was sacked as the manager. Another was the meeting at the university where my progress with my PhD was attacked.

The ordeal

The ordeal is a battle, the crucial battle, with a hostile force. Our fortunes are at a low, and we face defeat. Our fortunes look bleak. It is not clear that we will survive. Perhaps it will be the forces of evil that prevail.

This may sound melodramatic, but I suspect most people have faced such a moment (or more) in their career. In the myths, what sustains the hero is being true to him/herself and persevering, even when it appears that to do so will lead us directly to our death. At the same time, there may be something in the situation for the hero to learn. It may be courage, or being prepared to cooperate with others, or accepting that you can be wrong at times.

If the hero survives, it will be with the knowledge of that experience.

Reward

After the crisis, there is a reward. The dragon has been slain, the threat is over, and one can celebrate. A conflict may be resolved, and peace ensues. And the reward includes the hero's new knowledge and experience. One has attained greater understanding, and can deal with issues with more confidence and maturity.

Does this sound like a milestone in a career? Sometimes, a crisis can be resolved by a timely escape to a better place, or a strategy that out-manoeuvres the opposition. Sometimes, the enemy departs, and sometimes, a victory can be clear and decisive, bringing cleaner air all round.

There was a time like that at the centre for unemployed youth, when the unsavoury people were ousted and things went smoothly for a while. And I won increased respect from the people I was dealing with.

One reward that is precious in a career is increased autonomy because you are trusted and respected.

Residual issues

In the myth, not everything is resolved yet. There are residual issues that need to be addressed. But they can be faced with more confidence. We are moving into Act Three. The gods may still be angry, but the hero now knows how to deal with them.

Finally, the hero can see all the way back to the ordinary world from which he/she began. This is to say that the person can see the path they have come along, the events that have occurred along the way, and how their life connects back to the small child who wondered what they would ever do in life, and whether they would be successful.

Rebirth

The hero has yet to be ushered into this new life. In ancient times, the hunters and warriors had to be purified before they returned to the community, as they had blood on their hands. This is the last ordeal. It can be a second life-or-death experience where the hero is tested, to see if they really have learned the lessons of the test.

It is the final throes of the dark powers. If the hero endures, he/she is now transformed and can return to ordinary life as a new being with new insights. The legacy is new qualities such as calmness, peace, humility. Note, once more, that these are life qualities rather than job competencies.

Returning with the elixir

The point of this journey is that the hero gains the elixir, something essential and powerful that they were missing. It has been gained from their experiences in the dark worlds. The elixir has the power to heal. It can be treasure, literally, but it can also be knowledge, love and wisdom.

The hero also has the knowledge that the dark worlds can be survived. If nothing were brought back, the hero would be doomed to repeat the experience.

This is a framework that has countless variations. The important thing is that the journey is not merely about competence. It is also about self-development and morality. One starts out, either eager or reluctant, but one is deficient in some important values in life, and in undergoing the journey, one learns through the experience. For this to happen, one must immerse oneself in the journey completely, unreservedly.

"It needs to involve the heart in order for us to feel we have really found our place in life."

Hold to a firm inner vision, even as you adapt your plans. Development is gradual, like the growth of a tree on a mountain.

Allow the forces in the situation to fully act on you. In this way, you will comprehend the forces and master them. Achievement comes through insight.

Afterword

There are stages of our life when we think about a career. Using the lens of the mythological quest is one useful way to think about it. It offers guidelines that are useful: focus through a central, creative idea. Step outside the normal patterns of life. Find ways to realise things. And ultimately, find a liberating awareness of the whole of life.

You can see in the story of my life how I often felt that I was lost forever in terms of the goal of being a writer. Yet I had tried to do the right thing, I had tried to make my life worthwhile. I had tried to serve others. And at times, all I had was the idea to continue, to persevere, to be constant, to adhere to what is right. The message was, "This will bring success and the capacity to bring the situation to maturity."

And yet, there is a larger picture. A career is not all of life, it is a part. And our vision of what a career means is subject to the conditions of our life. In my family tree I have an ancestor who came from Germany to Australia just before World War II, so he was interned during the war. Along with him there were many other Germans. Most of them were not Nazi sympathisers, they were artists and craftsmen who had fled Germany in the 1930s.

These artists and craftsmen exercised their talents in the internment camp in whatever way was possible. They painted pictures on any piece of metal, Masonite or cardboard that came to hand. They painted their lives and the perseverance of their spirit. And in later years, the paintings were exhibited, and they bore testimony to the perseverance of spirit.

This is not what we consider to be the normal pathway of a career, but it is, in fact, something larger. The story of a career has to fold into the story of a worthy life.

References

Books

Elizabeth Arthur, 2020, *The Secret: Robert Martiensen*, Australian Scholarly Publishing, Melbourne.

Joseph Campbell, 1962, *The Masks of God: Oriental mythology*, Viking Press, New York.

Joseph Campbell, 1964, *The Masks of God: Occidental mythology*, Viking Press, New York.

Liz Greene & Julie Sharman-Burke, 1999, *The Mythic Journey: The meaning of myth as a guide for life*, Simon & Schuster, Sydney.

Annie Stewart, 2019, *Career to Calling: How to make the switch*, Impact Press, Sydney.

Christopher Vogler, 1998, *The Writer's Journey: Mythic structure for writers*, Second edition, Michael Wiese Production, Studio City CA.

Music (sleeve notes)

Richard Lockwood, 2012, *In the Doorway of the Dawn*, double CD, Chapter Music, Melbourne.

Tully, 1970 on vinyl, *Tully*, CD issued 2013 by Chapter Music, Melbourne.

Aside from the above references, there was material that Glenn developed on career development in his various jobs, which underpins the text in Part 3.

Author profile

Glenn Martin is the author of over thirty books. He is an independent scholar, researcher and writer. He has written books on ethics and values, the "bigger picture", family history, reflections on experience, and he has several volumes of poetry. His career includes teaching in high schools, tertiary institutions and adult education programs. He has managed organisations in the community sector, written commentary on employment law, management and training for professional publications, edited a national magazine for trainers, and designed online education courses. His current work is to write books.

Glenn lives in Sydney. He lived for twenty years in a valley in far north New South Wales, where he wrote two books of local history. He has five children and four grandchildren.

Other books by Glenn Martin

Stories/Reflections on experience

The Ten Thousand Things (2010)
Sustenance (2011)
To the Bush and Back to Business (2012)
The Big Story Falls Apart (2014)
The Quilt Approach: A Tasmanian Patchwork (2020)
Long Time Approaching: An Incomplete Memoir (2023)
Travel with a Pen (2023)
Library Meets Book Fair (2024)
The Traveller, Lost (2026)

Books on the bigger picture

Future: The Spiritual Story of Humanity (2020)
A Singular Book of Great Esteem: Life with the I Ching (2025)

Books on ethics and values

Human Values and Ethics in the Workplace (2010)
The Little Book of Ethics: A Human Values Approach (2011)
The Concise Book of Ethics (2012)
A Foundation for Living Ethically (2020)

Books on family history

A Modest Quest (2017)
The Search for Edward Lewis (2018)
They Went to Australia (2019)
No Gold in Melbourne: A Scottish Family in Australia (2021)
All the Rivers Come Together: Tracing Family (2022)
The Sailor, the Baron and the Dressmaker (2024)
Ordinary People, Remarkable Lives (2025)

Poetry collections

Flames in the Open (2007)
Love and Armour (2007)
Volume 4: I in the Stream (2017)
Volume 3: That Was Then: The Early Poems Project (2019)
The Way Is Open (2020)

Local history

Places in the Bush: A History of Kyogle Shire (1988)
The Kyogle Public School Centenary Book (1995)

www.ingramcontent.com/pod-product-compliance
Lightning Source LLC
LaVergne TN
LVHW012332100826
845148LV00017B/2114
9781764411431